Black Americans of Achievement

LEGACY EDITION

Ray Charles

MUSICIAN

Black Americans of Achievement

LEGACY EDITION

Muhammad Ali

Maya Angelou

Josephine Baker

George Washington Carver

Johnnie Cochran

Frederick Douglass

W.E.B. Du Bois

Marcus Garvey

Savion Glover

Alex Haley

Jimi Hendrix

Gregory Hines

Langston Hughes

Jesse Jackson

Scott Joplin

Coretta Scott King

Martin Luther King, Jr.

Malcolm X

Bob Marley

Thurgood Marshall

Barack Obama

Jesse Owens

Rosa Parks

Colin Powell

Condoleezza Rice

Chris Rock

Sojourner Truth

Harriet Tubman

Nat Turner

Booker T. Washington

Oprah Winfrey

Tiger Woods

Black Americans of Achievement

LEGACY EDITION

Ray Charles

MUSICIAN

Janet Hubbard-Brown

CHELSEA HOUSE
PUBLISHERS

An imprint of Infobase Publishing

Ray Charles

Copyright © 2008 by Infobase Publishing

Chelsea House
An imprint of Infobase Publishing
132 West 31st Street
New York NY 10001

Library of Congress Cataloging-in-Publication Data

Hubbard-Brown, Janet.
  Ray Charles / Janet Hubbard-Brown.
     p. cm. — (Black Americans of achievement : legacy edition)
  Includes bibliographical references (p.   ) and index.
  ISBN 978-1-60413-001-0 (hardcover)
  1. Charles, Ray, 1930-2004. 2. Singers—United States—Biography. I. Title.
ML420.C46H83 2008
782.42164092—dc22
[B]
                          2007052215

Chelsea House books are available at special discounts when purchased in bulk quantities for businesses, associations, institutions, or sales promotions. Please call our Special Sales Department in New York at (212) 967-8800 or (800) 322-8755.

You can find Chelsea House on the World Wide Web at
  http://www.chelseahouse.com

Series design by Keith Trego
Cover design by Keith Trego and Jooyoung An

Printed in the United States of America

Bang ML 10 9 8 7 6 5 4 3 2 1

This book is printed on acid-free paper.

All links and web addresses were checked and verified to be correct at the time of publication. Because of the dynamic nature of the web, some addresses and links may have changed since publication and may no longer be valid.

Contents

Two Crossover Songs

In 1958, 28-year-old Ray Charles and his touring band were playing for a dance in a town near Pittsburgh, Pennsylvania. Charles and his band had played for almost four hours, with one half-hour break. They still had about 15 minutes to go and had played through their entire repertory. Charles said in his autobiography, *Brother Ray: Ray Charles' Own Story*, "There was nothing left that I could think of, so I finally said to the band and the Raelettes [the chorus of three women who sang with him] 'Listen, I'm going to fool around and y'all just follow me.'"

He started the song with a riff, a short, repeated series of notes, and then he started singing, "Hey Mama don't you treat me wrong, Come and love your daddy all night long. . . ." To his surprise, the audience began to go wild. Charles later said he could feel "the whole room bouncing and shaking and carrying on something fierce." He had always taken pride in the fact that he never tested his songs on the public, preferring instead to be his own private testing service. But this experiment worked out. When they finished the song, later to be called, "What'd I Say," audience members ran up to ask where to buy the record.

COMBINING STYLES

Popular music in the early 1950s was segregated, as were the charts that kept the public up to date on which songs were hits. Whites listened to pop and country and western (called "hill-billy music" in the South), and blacks were tuned in to rhythm and blues (R&B). The rhythm came from swing jazz and the vocals reflected the blues. If the R&B sound received bad press, Charles took it personally, for he considered it "genuine, down-to-earth Negro music."

Rock and roll exploded onto the scene in 1955 with a song called "Rock Around the Clock." Rock and roll was a new form of music, a combination of the R&B and country and western genres. Added to the new style of music were instruments such as electrically amplified guitars, harmonicas, and drums. Early rock and roll hits were often R&B songs covered by white artists. For example, a white band, Bill Haley and His Comets, cleaned up the lyrics to Big Joe Turner's song "Shake, Rattle and Roll" and made it a hit on the pop charts. Turner's version was a hit on the R&B chart.

From the beginning of his career, Ray Charles fused the sounds of gospel with the rhythm patterns of the blues (which was essentially black pop music) and began to slowly break down the barriers between sacred and secular music. Blind since the age of six and orphaned as a teenager, Charles had turned to music, putting all of his emotions into song. At 28 years old, he was already married and a father and had been on the road for five years. He had also put out 20 singles (14 of them medium to major hits) under an African-American recording company called Atlantic Records, plus 4 albums that boasted strong sales.

Legendary musician Ray Charles revolutionized popular music in the mid twentieth century. By fusing the sounds of gospel, R&B, rock and roll, and country music, he aided in the creation of the soul genre, which would influence music for generations to come.

Charles's recording of "I Got a Woman" in 1954 is often said to be the first soul record. It and "Hallelujah I Love Her So" made it to the top of the R&B chart. His "Drown in My Own Tears" was number one on the R&B chart in 1956. Sung in Charles's soulful and raspy voice and accompanied by piano and horns, these songs did not cross over to the white pop charts.

SPONTANEOUS EXPLOSION

After the success of "I Got a Woman," Charles wanted to create a "crossover" song, one that would appeal equally to blacks and whites, but he knew that no one could guess which song would become a hit. As the 1950s drew to a close, the taste of the youth of both races was undergoing radical changes. They liked listening to each other's music, as did the musicians who made the music. White parents were horrified at the music their kids were listening and dancing to, but there was no going back.

Responding to the audience's overwhelming reception of "What'd I Say," Charles and the Raelettes recorded the song in 1959. Tom Dowd, the recording engineer at Atlantic Records, did not think it was all that special at the time. "Three or four takes, and it was done," he said. The producers knew when they heard the final result, though, that they had something big on their hands. *New York Times* writer Bob Herbert wrote in 2004,

> Ray opened fire on two very distinct cultures at one and the same time: the white-bread mass culture that was on its guard against sexuality of any kind (and especially the black

IN HIS OWN WORDS...

Soul is when you take a song and make it part of you—a part that's so true, so real, people think it must have happened to you. . . . It's like electricity: we don't really know what it is, do we? But it's a force that can light a room. Soul is like electricity, like a spirit, a drive, a power.

Quoted in Michael Lydon, *Ray Charles: Man and Music.* New York: Routledge, 2004.

kind), and the black religious community, which felt that gospel was the Lord's music, and thus should be off-limits to the wild secular shenanigans that Ray represented.

Michael Lydon described the song in his book, *Ray Charles: Man and Music*:

> The track was over seven and a half minutes long and strangely asymmetrical: Ray hammering fuzzy bass riffs on electric piano for a half-dozen choruses, finally singing a grab bag of blues clichés that tell no story. The horns join him at last, and after building to a climax of "What'd I say" repeated over and over, Ray and the band stop.
>
> Immediately a gaggle of men and women's voices rise in protest. They want the music to keep going. And though pretending he doesn't understand, Ray starts again, this time singing a long "Unnnnh" to which the ladies respond "Unnnnh." Then a long "Ohhhhh" from Ray, and a long "Ohhhhh" response from the ladies, then faster and faster. . . .

Dowd and the producers at Atlantic Records were not quite sure what to do with the edited track. After toning it down a little, they finally decided to release it in the summer, when teenagers would listen to their music on the beach. When released in 1959, the song was banned by several radio stations because it was considered too suggestive, but young audiences were enthralled. "What'd I Say" went to number two on the black chart and number six on the white chart.

GREATER SUCCESS

In the meantime, Charles was wooed to a much bigger player in the field, recording company ABC-Paramount. They offered him the most money any black musician had ever received and assured him that he could eventually own his master recordings (the owner of the master recordings, usually the studio, could make significant profits).

At ABC-Paramount, Charles began to put together an album of place songs—tunes that describe geographic locations—that eventually became the album *Genius Hits the Road*. He liked the 1930 classic song written by Hoagy Carmichael titled "Georgia on My Mind" and decided to include it. It took 20 takes to record it, and tears streamed down his face throughout. Every note was packed with emotion. It became the most popular record in America, hitting number one on the *Billboard* list at the end of 1960 and becoming one of Charles's signature songs.

Two years after the concert that launched "What'd I Say," a teenager named David Ritz drove from Dallas to Fort Worth, Texas, to hear the singer who was often referred to as the "High Priest," Ray Charles. An eight-piece band played the first hour. Only 20 or 30 other white faces could be spotted in a sea of black fans who, according to Ritz, were "dressed in shocking pink, Popsicle orange, Wizard of Oz green." He described Charles, who was then 30 years old, as he walked onto the stage: "From afar, his sunglasses look like a bandage hiding some mysterious pain. When he comes closer, the glasses appear to be sewn into his face. He is twitching and laughing.... He opens his mouth and the spirits come charging out, like convicts escaping prison." (Ritz would later become a writer and was chosen by Charles to ghostwrite his autobiography years later.) The song "What'd I Say," which by this time had become the hottest song in the country, brought the crowd to its feet in a kind of ecstasy.

Michael Lydon wrote that "What'd I Say" was "different, wildly sexy, and fabulously danceable.... It became the life of a million parties, the spark of as many romances, a song to date the summer by. It brought Ray Charles to everybody." Of "Georgia On My Mind," Lydon wrote, "With [this song] Ray began to plumb not only the black American soul, but the soul of the country." Charles's two crossover songs could not have been more different, one a wild dance number and the other a poignant ballad. In 1963, the last rhythm and blues chart was published. The charts were no longer segregated by race.

Although he would record pop and country and western albums, Charles's soulful songs, derived from a deep hollow of personal loss and suffering, were the most authentic representation of his own life. He explained to a *Time* magazine reporter in 1968 what soul meant to him: "It's a force that can light a room. The force radiates from a sense of selfhood, a sense of knowing where you've been and what it means. Soul is a way of life—but it's always the hard way." His songs tell his life story, which started in a small Southern town in the grip of poverty.

2

A Tragic Beginning

"When I say we were poor, I'm spelling it with a capital P," Ray Charles wrote in his autobiography, *Brother Ray: Ray Charles' Own Story.* "Even compared to other blacks in Greensville, we were on the bottom of the ladder looking up at everyone else. Nothing below us 'cept the ground."

Charles's father, Bailey Robinson, came to Greenville, Florida (which locals pronounced "Greensville"), 50 miles east of Tallahassee, in the 1920s. He moved there from Albany, Georgia, along with his mother and his wife, Mary Jane Robinson. Bailey was at least six feet tall and muscular, a physical laborer who worked at a sawmill pulling logs into the skidder or laying track for the railroad. Mary Jane stacked planks at the sawmill. In Greenville, the Robinsons took in a young woman named Aretha (nicknamed Retha) Williams for a time after her mother died. Williams then moved to Albany to stay with friends, and there, on September 23, 1930, she gave birth to a baby boy she named Ray Charles Robinson. The townspeople later learned that the father was Bailey Robinson.

Williams returned to Greenville with her baby, whom everyone called RC, a few months later. They lived in a section of Greenville called "Jellyroll," which was made up of a few small houses and tar-paper shacks built by transient workers. The more prosperous blacks lived in Blackbottom, closer to the center of Greenville. The main industries in the town were cotton, lumber, and cattle.

Eventually Bailey and Mary Jane Robinson separated; Bailey married a woman named Stella and moved to the town of Shamrock. Mary Jane remained close with Retha Williams, and after her little boy, Jabbo, died, she came to think of RC as a son.

In the 1930s, the United States was in the middle of the Great Depression and earning a living was tough, even for the educated. Retha Williams had no education beyond fifth grade and was sickly. She and her little boy were well liked by their neighbors, though. Some of the women who had businesses taking in laundry from whites began to turn over some of the extra work to her.

When RC was one year old, Retha Williams gave birth to another son, whom she named George. No one knew who the father was. Williams was one of the poorest residents in the black quarter, so the townspeople helped as much as they could. She was strict with her two sons, but RC adored her and later took pride in telling people how she never drank, smoked, or swore.

On Saturday nights, the locals often met at Mr. Pit's Red Wing Café, where owner Wiley Pitman, nicknamed Mr. Pit, played piano. A jukebox and a piano were placed against one wall of the café, and the people of Jellyroll have memories of RC either playing piano or listening to music from the jukebox. Charles liked to recall the first time he heard Mr. Pit playing boogie-woogie on the piano, when he was three years old: He ran into the café, and Mr. Pit picked him up and allowed him to run his fingers up and down the keyboard. From that moment, Mr. Pit became a teacher to RC, teaching him to pick out a melody with one finger. It cost five cents to play the jukebox, and soon RC had a special seat on a bench beside it where he would sit for hours, listening. Because he did not have money, he listened to the music that the café patrons selected, which included blues, big band, and boogie-woogie.

Wiley Pitman and his wife, Miz Georgia, created a small general store in the café where they sold beer, pigs' feet, salt, and flour, among other supplies. They also ran a boarding-house to accommodate the watermelon pickers who came in droves during the summer. When Retha Williams could not take care of him, the Pitmans adopted little George. Williams and RC lived in a shack behind the café, though, so the brothers were able to spend time together.

The two brothers were inseparable. They became a familiar sight as they ran around the yards playing their games. By the time they were five and four, their mother had them chopping wood and hauling water. Every Sunday, without fail, she took them to church, where preachers fired up the congregation with emotional sermons that brought people to tears and shouts of joy. RC loved the gospel singing in church.

It was obvious early on that the boys were fascinated by mechanical things. George was good at math and liked to make toys from wood scraps, and RC had a talent for taking things apart and putting them back together. It was predicted that they were do well at Greenville Training School, the local school for black children.

TRAGEDY STRIKES

On a hot summer day when the boys were five and four, they were jumping in and out of a big washtub to cool off. Retha Williams was inside her shack, ironing. George jumped into the washtub to fetch a penny he saw on the bottom, but soon began to thrash around. RC realized that something was wrong and tried to pull his brother out, but he wasn't strong enough. Screaming, he raced inside to get his mother. She came running and lifted George out. She shook him, rubbed him, and tried to breathe life back into him, but he was dead.

Everyone grieved for George, but for RC, it was a loss that he would never get over. When Charles wrote about it later, he said it "was my first real taste of tragedy, and even after more than forty years, the taste hasn't left my mouth."

A few months later, RC's eyes began to tear up. His mother soon realized that the substance wasn't tears, but a thick mucus, which was not a good sign. Charles wrote in his autobiography, "Faraway distances were fading. I was like a guy who stands on top of a mountain and one week sees fifteen miles off, the next week only ten miles, the third week only five. At first, I could still make out large forms, then only colors, then only night from day." Williams took RC to a doctor in nearby Madison and was told that he was going blind. There was nothing they could do. Years later, doctors guessed that it was an eye disease called "congenital glaucoma" that caused the blindness. That was the medical diagnosis, but some people didn't think it too farfetched to assume that the shock and guilt of watching his brother drown contributed to RC's blindness.

It horrified Williams to think of what could happen to a grown disabled black man in the South. She made up her mind that her son would not be crippled by his disability. Her first thought was that he had to learn to care for himself. With that in mind, she made him continue to do his chores—scrubbing floors and bringing in water—and encouraged him to get to know all the paths and roads in Greenville. When their neighbors criticized her methods, she replied, "He's blind, but he ain't stupid. He's lost his sight, but he ain't lost his mind." She taught him math and the alphabet, but she knew that wasn't enough. The teachers at the Greenville Training School had never had to deal with a blind child, so sending him to school there was not an option.

Williams went to the white postmistress and to the local doctor for advice, but help was closer than that. One of her friends, Mitty King, cooked for a white family named the Reamses. A.D. Reams owned a big store in town and his wife, Ruth, taught Sunday school at the Baptist church. Williams was told to bring the boy to the Reamses' house, where RC played piano for them. The Reamses decided that they wanted to help, and A.D. Reams found out that the Florida School for the Deaf and Blind in St. Augustine had a department for colored children. RC could begin as soon as they could get him there. The best news was that the state would pay his tuition.

RC begged to stay home, however, and Mary Jane Robinson took his side. But Williams refused to be sentimental, even

Charles's Blindness

When Ray Charles went blind at age seven, his mother was determined not to let her little boy succumb to his disability. Charles said, "When I got to feeling sorry for myself, she'd get tough and say, 'you're blind, you ain't dumb; you lost your sight not your mind.'" Charles's mother was criticized for making Ray do chores and for allowing him to explore the town on his own, but she ignored the naysayers.

Stories abound about Charles's ability to "see." In 1953, a group of musicians in New Orleans told Charles to meet them at a bar. They watched, stunned, as he walked down four city blocks, crossed a street, and entered the bar where they were waiting for him. One of them asked Charles how he did it. He responded, "Easy. I do just like a bat. You notice I wear hard-heeled shoes? I listen to the echo from my heels, and that way I know where there's a wall. When I hear a space, that's the open door."

When in Florida in 1955, Charles's band manager, Jeff Brown, told a promoter that Charles could shoot a pistol. The promoter did not believe it, and Brown bet him $20 that Charles could hit two out of five cans. They set up the empty cans out in a field, and Brown handed Charles the gun. He stood though it must have been hard on her. She and her baby had never been apart. Still, she boldly put her only little boy on the train to St. Augustine and asked the conductor to watch out for him. RC sat by himself, drowning in grief. He was seven years old.

Although St. Augustine was only 160 miles from home, for RC it could have been 1,000. He cried every day. Charles later wrote in his autobiography, "Downhearted and lonely, scared, nervous, and unsure of myself, I finally realized I had no choice." The 15-acre campus consisted of a dozen wooden buildings. RC was sent to the South Campus. He learned quickly that the school was rigidly segregated and that the whites lived in much better circumstances on the North Campus.

The classrooms on the South Campus were crowded. Boys' and girls' dormitories, an auditorium, the dining room, laundry, and a residence for black employees were all under one

behind Charles and threw the cans into the air. Charles aimed and fired when a can hit the ground, hitting the cans three out of five times.

Charles rarely complained about his blindness, but Ruth Robinson said that, during the 1970s, "Ray was bitter about everything. Especially about being blind. He'd deny it, but he felt trapped by blindness. With sight, he figured, he could have been a lawyer, an engineer, or become a bigger star."

Toward the end of his life he was asked by *New York Times* reporters Jon Pareles and Bernard Weinraub what effect blindness had on his career and he replied, "Nothing, nothing, nothing. I was going to do what I was going to do anyway. I played music since I was 3. I could see then. I lost my sight when I was 7. So blindness didn't have anything to do with it. It didn't give me anything. And it didn't take nothing."

In 1994, the American Foundation for the Blind (AFB) presented Charles with the first Helen Keller Personal Achievement Award because of his determination not to allow his disability to limit him. According to the AFB, the award was created to honor individuals who have significantly improved the lives of people who are blind or visually impaired.

roof. Whites enjoyed the 11 other multipurpose buildings on the North Campus. There were 90 black students and 300 or more white students. African-American children learned quickly that they would be wise not to make any trouble. As an adult looking back on those days, Charles wrote, "it's awfully strange thinking about separating small children—black from white—when most of 'em can't even make out the difference between the two colors."

The black members of the faculty at the school were dedicated to their young charges. RC caught up quickly—he easily learned Braille, the art of reading with the fingertips—but he remained unhappy. He had started six weeks later than the other kids and was teased for not having any shoes and for crying for his mother. RC dreamed of Christmas, when he would see his mother again. At the last minute, though, Williams could not get the money together to bring him home and he had to stay on campus. He was the only child left behind. He wandered around the campus for two weeks, crying his heart out. By the time the other kids returned, he was thrilled to have them back.

Then another problem arose. RC's right eye was causing severe pain. The doctor said that they had to cut the eye out, which terrified the little boy. He had the operation in the winter and was able to attend a few classes before summer break.

The thrill of going home for summer outweighed all the awful things that had happened to him. When he got off the train, he ran into his mother's arms and they went home to Jellyroll, where everyone came out to greet RC. Two ladies at church had pianos, and they invited him in to play every Sunday afternoon. The rest of the time he played with his friends.

All too soon, RC was back at school living a regimented life. There were 60 deaf and blind boys who slept in one large open room. They were awakened by a bell at 5:30 A.M., and breakfast was served at 6:40. The boys lined up, the blind along one wall,

By the age of seven, Ray Charles Robinson was completely blind. His mother was determined to provide him with the best possible opportunities, so she sent him to the Florida School for the Deaf and the Blind, which at the time was one of the few places that had a department for black children. This photograph shows the entrance to the school in 2002.

the deaf against the other. The deaf led the way into the dining room, and one of the blind boys said the blessing. They went to chapel at 8:00 A.M., and classes started at 9:00. At 4:00 they could play, usually the blind with the blind and the deaf with the deaf. The blind boys loved to play Score Ball, a game in which they would bat a rolled-up newspaper, winning points if it hit the fence. They ran to where they heard it land and then swept the ground with the bat until they found it. Sometimes after dinner, RC would don coveralls and join some of the others who put together brooms to be sold by the school.

RC lived for night, when, after his homework was done, he could listen to the jazz station, WFOY, on the radio. The children weren't allowed to get into bed until a certain time, so he would curl up on the trunk in front of his bed and enter the world of jazz.

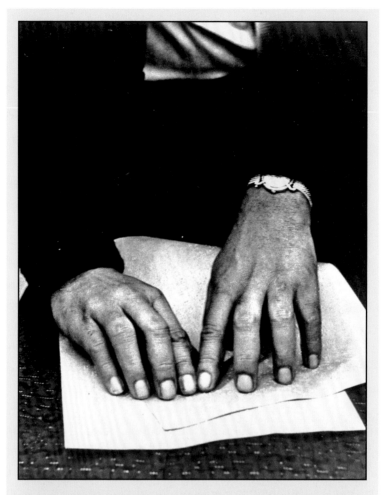

At the Florida School for the Deaf and the Blind, Ray Charles learned how to read Braille. He is shown here reading Braille as an adult. Braille is a system by which many blind people are able to read. Each braille character is made up of six dot positions arranged in a rectangle. Letters are distinguished by feeling which dots are raised.

At the school, RC was known as a mischievous boy, but he was often blamed for things he didn't do. A fast learner, he usually had to wait for others to catch up. He excelled in math, disliked English, and learned to type 75 words per minute on a typewriter. In his second year at the school, when he was eight, RC knew he wanted to be a musician. One of the teachers, Mrs. Lawrence, taught him European classical music. He learned harmony and keyboard techniques and started to play Chopin, Mozart, and other masters. Mrs. Lawrence also taught him to read music in Braille. It was difficult, though: He needed to play the left-hand part while reading the Braille with the right hand, then switch, and finally combine the two.

As he grew older, RC sang in the South Campus chorus and spent time with the jazz group. It gave him a new status to be able to play an instrument, because popular music, jazz, and blues were what the kids liked to talk about. There was only one practice piano on the campus (the good one was used only for special occasions), and this created sharp competition among the boys. Competition grew particularly intense between RC and his friend James Kendrick. Once, James made RC promise him a turn at the piano after 15 minutes. When his time was up, RC removed all the keys and carried them up to his room in a bag.

By age 12, RC was the school's most talented musician, and he played and sang popular songs when the South Campus Literary Society had its weekly gatherings. RC also had the school rocking at the annual Christmas party one year when he trained five boys to be back-up singers for the song "Jingle Bell Boogie." He didn't have to spend another lonely Christmas at the school, as the staff chipped in to get him home.

RC sometimes found it hard to be the only blind kid in Greenville, but his mother would not put up with his self-pity. She kept pushing him forward and stressed that knowledge was the key to his future. She told him often that she might not always be around and that he had to be independent. She also insisted that he always tell the truth and that, if he wanted something, he had better be willing to work for it. He learned to ride a bicycle one summer, guiding himself by sound and the feel of the tires on pavement and dirt. As RC and his friends grew into adolescents, however, they were like any other teens who felt at loose ends. They were barely aware of the war that was happening across the ocean, which would come to be known as World War II.

During the 1940s, a couple named Alice and Henry Johnson invited RC to visit them where they lived in the black section of Tallahassee, called "Frenchtown." They had owned a store in Jellyroll, and RC helped out in their store in Tallahassee. He liked Tallahassee, especially the music he heard there. The members of the Johnsons' social club bought RC a clarinet, and, at age 13, he joined a band called Lawyer Smith and His Band. The band was booked into all kinds of places, from cafés to weddings to roadhouses. Each New Year's Eve, they played at the Governor's Ball at the state capitol. RC loved the atmosphere of music, smoke, and laughter.

When RC returned to school, he explored the streets of St. Augustine and began to play piano for ladies' social clubs and tea parties, all approved by the school. He also began to rebel. When he disobeyed rules or acted up, the teachers would forbid him to go into the music room. He grew restless. A new teacher arrived and tried a new tactic: She made him a dorm monitor. He was satisfied again.

Then came the phone call that would send him spiraling into a world of pain. His mother had died, the caller said, and RC must go home right away. "Nothing had hit me like that," RC recalled years later, "Not George drowning. Not going blind. Nothing." Retha Williams was 31 when she died. The doctor thought she might have eaten a spoiled sweet potato pie, but others thought she had been sick for a long time. Everyone began to worry about RC, who seemed unreachable in his grief. He was to say later, "I sat alone, silent, not moving a muscle or saying a word. Not crying, not eating, not praying. My mind just drifted somewhere out there in space."

Ma Beck, a midwife and medicine woman in her sixties, came to see the grief-stricken teenager. She had known his mother well and had doctored her over the years. She said to RC, "Your mama spent her whole life preparing you for this here day. You gotta carry on. That's all there is to it. That's what she'd want. And that's what you gotta do. You gotta carry on, RC." These were the words that finally got to RC, and he broke down and sobbed for hours.

At his mother's funeral, he touched her face and said goodbye. He spent the summer alone. He went to Tallahassee and played in Lawyer's band, but the entire time he was thinking about what he was going to do. He went back to school, and because of a foolish prank was stripped of his dorm monitor position. The school wanted to expel him, but he defiantly quit instead. He was completely alone in the world.

3

On the Road, Age 16

Mary Jane Robinson had friends in Jacksonville, Florida, a bigger city than either St. Augustine or Tallahassee. She suggested that RC visit them, so he took the train 50 miles north to meet Fred and Lena Thompson, who had agreed to give him a room. The Thompsons, who were childless, were happy to have RC move in, and he enjoyed their company, as well. On Saturday nights, they gathered around the radio to listen to the Grand Ole Opry; on Sundays, they listened to *Amos 'n Andy*.

The Thompsons offered to help RC financially, but he was determined to make it through his music. Fred Thompson suggested that RC join the musician's union, so he went downtown to Local 632, where members sat and chatted around an old upright piano three stories above a mission. RC showed up daily, announcing that he was ready to play and sing. The other musicians smiled at his innocence; some of them had been sitting there waiting to play for as long as two weeks.

LEARNING BY DOING

At that time, it was common for music performers to become stranded in different towns. They would sit on the union hall benches until somebody called for players. The "booker" would call for a saxophone or a piano, and whoever was there would take off. This involved a lot of waiting.

The world of classical music was mostly closed to blacks, although many of them had been trained to play that way. Black players were associated with popular music, and they played country clubs and society events in the white world. The music they played had roots in everything from slave songs and spirituals to Bach and old English folk songs.

RC decided to enroll in the only school available to him— the company of professional musicians. According to author Michael Lydon:

> Pop music didn't speed up and slow down like classical music; players sank deep into the unchanging backbeat groove, one TWO three FOUR, one TWO three FOUR, that gave the music its African, hand-clap rhythm. A feeling for "blue notes" ran in RC's blood, but he still needed to learn just how to use those aching African tones, bent between major and minor, to give the plainest melody a tragic twist, tint the plainest harmony with the red-purples of a southern sunset.

RC listened carefully but realized that he couldn't memorize every pop song. Much more important was to learn certain forms, repeated often, that shaped the pop songs. It was like learning all the songs at once. The blues, which consisted of 12 African-rooted measures that rocked endlessly back and forth from keynote to dominant note, and the 32-bar standard (the Americanized version of the European art song that usually ran in an A-A-B-A pattern) were the primary forms that would send any musician on his way. The musicians also had to learn how to jump in and stay on track while others were improvising.

RC was filled with ambition, and he practiced every chance he got. The older musicians around the union hall were happy to show him new chords, and he loved the jam sessions, which were like boot camp for new musicians. They were a form of combat in which you either stomped or were stomped. One musician would change the tempo of a song they all knew, and everyone was expected to follow. That meant changing keys as the lead musician might switch from swing to a Latin beat.

RC soon became discouraged by the lack of available work, but in a couple of days he would go back to the union hall. He learned to see music as war, and once he understood that, he began to understand his own strengths. For example, he had perfect pitch. According to Lydon, he could "hear the whole combo and each instrument's distinct voice at the same time." Before long, he was holding his own with the veterans.

Eventually, RC was given work as a substitute at Manuel's Tap Room, where he also could look for work at higher-end clubs. Soon, he was playing in drummer Henry Washington's big band, which consisted of five saxophones, four trombones, four trumpets, and piano, guitar, bass, and drums for rhythm. He loved the big band sound; he could paint all the sound colors that belonged to pop music. He decided that, one day, he would have a big band of his own.

EARLY MUSICAL INFLUENCES

By the end of World War II in 1945, small bands were cropping up all over the country. Lyrics were important to the pros with whom RC played, which made the small bands with their crazy chords and superfast tempos a little too wild for the players in Jacksonville. This music was called "bebop."

In 1946, three small bands, all of them black, became leaders of American pop music: the Nat "King" Cole Trio, Louis Jordan & His Tympany Five, and Johnny Moore's Three Blaz-

As a young adult, Charles was a great fan of Nat "King" Cole and his trio. Charles attempted to emulate Cole's singing and style of music. Here, Cole (right) poses with the other members of the trio, Wesley Prince (left) and Oscar Moore (center) in 1943.

ers. All catered to the white ideal of a black person, who was graceful and musical and knew his place. The leaders of each of the bands played instruments and sang.

The jazz-blues of Cole and the Three Blazers appealed to RC the most, and in fact he had been a big fan of Cole's in the Greenville days. The groups' music had RC dreaming big: If they could do it, he could. He began to imitate Cole, trying to fit his piano fills around his voice ("fills" describe the countermelody used to fill an empty measure in the music) and working on the precise diction of Cole, which meant making his throat and jaw tighter than was natural for him. Henry Washington liked what RC was doing and so did the audience in Jacksonville. They thought it cute the way the blind boy could sound exactly like his idols. Even as he emulated Cole, RC was not aware that his "acting suave despite the pain of segregation gave Cole bleeding ulcers and a three-pack-a-day smoking habit."

In 1946, RC turned 16. He was still shy, and most nights he returned to the Thompsons' house. His friend Tiny York was putting together a band to tour around central Florida, though, and asked RC to join him as pianist with his own featured spot. RC was enthusiastic about the project. Some of the older performers quickly became jealous of the kid who had been given a starring role, but there wasn't much they could do about it—although they did retaliate by making him sit on a soda crate during the long drives.

ON HIS OWN

It wasn't long before York's band was losing ground. The band members decided to return to Jacksonville, but RC announced that he was staying in Orlando, one of the stops on the tour. His decision revealed a part of his character that would remain with him the rest of his life: When he had to choose between dependence and independence, he chose the latter. He had been through a great deal, and one of the lessons in his mind was that, ultimately, humans live and die alone. It was best not to depend on anyone.

RC had a room at a boarding house, and he would go out to explore the city, which had a population of 55,000—15,000 of them black. RC looked for work at Orlando's top black nightclub, the Sunshine Club, and at the South Street Casino, but was told to come back later. For days he went without food. He attached himself to a group of musicians who weren't much better off than he was, but he did get occasional meals from their families. During this period, he heard that his father had died. Since he had not really known Bailey Robinson, the news hardly had any effect on him.

Finally, in 1947, things began to change. A man named Joe Anderson was head of the band at the Sunshine Club, and he

called RC to come and play. RC offered to write some arrangements, and Anderson took him up on it. RC couldn't write
down the notes, so he started by working out complete charts
in his head and then dictated every voice to another musician, describing what he wanted each instrument to play. The
musicians in town were impressed. RC's music worked on the
bandstand, and with the money he made from this job, he was
able to afford a record player. He began to listen to the greats:
Ella Fitzgerald, Billie Holiday, Dizzy Gillespie, and Charlie
Parker.

RC amazed his friends with his ability to run around town,
use pay phones, and even ride a bicycle. Then the day arrived
when he was asked to audition for Lucky Millinder. If accepted,
he could go on a national tour. He didn't make it, though, and
it broke his heart. His pride was also hurt, and to make up for
it, he began to practice the piano for hours at a time. As with
his other hurts, the rejection left a scar that stayed with him
for the rest of his life.

At that point, Orlando had lost its appeal. RC agreed when
one of his pals suggested that they go to Tampa.

TAMPA: A THRIVING BLACK COMMUNITY

As young as he was, RC had met a lot of fellow musicians while
touring around Florida. On his arrival in Tampa, he ran into
Gossie D. McKee, who had played at the Two-Spot, a dance
palace in Jacksonville. McKee, a native of Tampa, knew everybody. Before long, he helped RC find positions in two bands
and a room in a boardinghouse run by two sisters. RC was
hired as pianist with the first band, Charlie Brantley's Honey-
drippers. One of the horn players remembered him as being
talented but not a standout; however, he did stand out in the
white country band he joined, the Florida Playboys, which was
made up of older white musicians. Though it was unusual for
an African American to play in a country band, Charles always
recalled the stint fondly. He started to make enough money

to send some to A.D. Reams, who looked after RC's savings account at the Bank of Greenville.

RC was 17 when he met 16-year-old Louise Mitchell and they fell madly in love. When her parents tried to force them to break up, the couple hopped a bus to Miami. Her parents finally relented and told them that they could live together if they returned to Tampa. The couple agreed to the terms and rented an apartment for three dollars a week.

Soon, RC was booked with the Manzy Harris Orchestra at the Skyhaven Club, which catered to wealthy whites. RC became a minor local star and began to make good money. The band members were happy there—some felt that they could stay there forever—but RC's friend Gossie McKee had bigger dreams. He talked to RC about the world up north, where no one cared about skin color. He also told RC that he

Dealing with Discrimination

Racism was so accepted in Greenville that Charles never thought much about it. When he went to the School for the Deaf and Blind, at age seven, however, he was much more aware of a racial divide. One of the saddest statements he ever uttered was during a 1970 interview with *Playboy Magazine*. He said, "Being blind was easy compared to being black in America," he said. "The greatest handicap I've had—and still have—is my color."

When Charles was in his twenties and having some success in the music world, an incident occurred that convinced him to leave the South for Seattle. A small group of white girls who admired Charles's band wanted to meet them after a show. They had to hide on the floor of the car because of the danger in which it would put the black musicians if the girls were seen partying with them.

In 2004, Jon Pareles and Bernard Weinraub quoted Charles as saying, "What I never understood to this day, to this very day, was how white people could have black people cook for them, make their meals, but wouldn't let them sit at the table with them. How can you dislike someone so much and have them cook for you? Shoot, if I don't like someone you ain't cooking nothing for me, ever."

could come up with some high-paying gigs anywhere in the United States.

RC was torn. He knew that all the music he heard on radio and records came from big Northern cities, yet he did not want to leave the little home he had created with Louise. He also knew that her family would not allow her to leave with him. Still, the two young men continued to discuss where they might go. New York and Chicago came up often, but both thought those cities were too big.

Gossie McKee had met a girl in Canada, but he did not mention her to RC. When she wrote to him that she was moving to Seattle, however, he worked harder at persuading RC to go with him. Two weeks later, RC and Gossie McKee bought one-way bus tickets to Seattle. RC backed out at the last minute, but McKee decided to go. He took RC's precious records

Shows all over the country were usually segregated until the Civil Rights Act was passed in 1964. In 1961 in Atlanta, blacks had to use a back entrance to hear performers like Nat "King" Cole and Duke Ellington. The stars who were booked for those shows tried to show sympathy, but they had to earn money, so most of them accepted the rules and went on. When Charles was scheduled to appear at a college in Augusta, Georgia, the student president sent him a telegram to tell him that the dance floor was only open to whites. Charles made a spontaneous decision to refuse to play under those conditions. He told his agent, Milt Shaw, that he would not do any more segregated gigs. Charles received positive publicity for taking that stand.

Charles gave an interview for a show called *Of Black America*, a CBS special that focused on black achievement. He said that black music was "loose" and that "you play what you feel." It was important, he said, not to lose the heart and soul of a song when cleaning it up for white audiences. He invested lyrics with a double meaning, like "singing about the woman, but you are really also talking about all the kicking around you've had."

Even as Ray Charles became a big star, he was still hampered by the effects of racial discrimination in the United States. Above, a police officer in Jackson, Mississippi, places a segregation sign in front of a train station in 1956. For Charles and the members of his band, signs like this were very common.

and clothes, so RC had to follow. When Louise learned what was going on, she clung to RC, and he promised to send for her as soon as he could. For the trip, he withdrew $500 from his savings account, money that no one knew he had.

SEATTLE

The first thing RC noticed when arriving at the Seattle bus terminal was that whites and blacks waited together in one room.

McKee came to pick up RC and, after giving him something to eat, took him to the Black and Tan, the oldest black nightclub in Seattle. Before RC knew it, he and McKee were being introduced to the audience as musicians ready to play. McKee said later, "We stepped up there and we went into all the pretty tunes we'd been doing at Drew Field. The people went wild, and this was our very first night! Before we left, Gus West, who ran the Elks Club, came up and offered us a gig. We could hardly believe our ears."

The Northwest at that time was "one big scene," according to bassist Traf Hubert. RC took Seattle by storm. He and McKee rented rooms from a woman named Georgia Kemp. The song "Georgia on My Mind" had already been released by Hoagy Carmichael, and RC liked to hum it when Kemp entered the room. He finally was able to send for Louise after leaving those rooms and renting a house on a hillside overlooking Lake Washington.

RC and Gossie McKee became so popular at the Elks Club that the manager of the Rocking Chair, a more upscale club, offered them a job. They needed to find a bassist to complete their trio and found 24-four-year-old Milton Garrett. Garrett had a big sound and beat, but he was also known all around as a big drinker and heroin addict and had been jailed for assault and rape. McKee wanted to try someone else, but RC liked Garrett's sound. They called themselves McSon Trio, for McKee and Robinson, and they wore matching navy blue double-breasted suits. At McKee's suggestion, RC started to wear sunglasses to hide his deformed eye. The sunglasses became a trademark. At the time, RC was only 18 years old. Biographer Lydon described RC at this age:

> He does not look blind; his eyes could have just blinked shut. His smile conveys both the shyness and the self-confidence of youth, and he has a youth's thin moustache and trace of beard. The ears are high and prominent, the jaw and neck strong, but overall there is a lightness to the head

that suggests a slender figure. The picture could be from any high school yearbook, of a fellow who could be both valedictorian and class cutup, best dancer and best debater, his motto "Baby, the C stands for charm!"

McKee bought a 15-minute spot on the radio on Saturday afternoons, and soon university students were calling in wanting more. A 15-year-old named Quincy Jones who dreamed of arranging music met RC, and RC became his idol. Jones's gratitude for RC's tutoring and his enthusiasm got through the wall RC put up around himself when working with most musicians, and they became good friends. Both were on their way to stardom, and everyone knew it.

In his personal life, however, there were problems. Louise was homesick, and the couple began to fight often. She had had a miscarriage and was heartbroken over it. McKee's and RC's relationship was changing, too. RC would head out to jam sessions after they were done at the Rocking Chair, but McKee went home so he could be up early to find more work for the trio. He also knew that Milt Garrett and his friends were using drugs. RC was intrigued and asked them to let him try, but they held back, concerned about his youth and his blindness. Like any adolescent who wants to fit in, though, he was determined. He started out trying marijuana but soon moved to shooting up heroin. He was convinced that he could control his drug use.

DISCOVERED

A musician from Los Angeles named Jackie McVea heard RC play and rushed back to L.A. to tell everybody about the blind man who could bring down the house with his playing. Weeks later, Jack Lauderdale, the president of a small record company called Down Beat Records out of Los Angeles, came to hear the trio play and offered them a deal to make a record. RC was thrilled; as usual, McKee remained skeptical. Lauderdale didn't like RC's name, however. "Ray Robinson" wouldn't work either, because people could mix it up with the name of boxer Sugar Ray Robinson. He suggested Ray Charles, and it stuck. The trio made the recording in Seattle, and Lauderdale was pleased.

Lauderdale was true to his word, and the record arrived in the mail. To the astonishment of the trio, Charles's song "Confession Blues" hit the charts, peaking at number five on *Billboard*'s Best Selling Retail Race Records—the black chart (shortly thereafter, the chart was renamed Best Selling Retail Rhythm & Blues Records). He and McKee went right to work to produce more songs, but changes were in the offing. Lauderdale gave the trio a contract and flew McKee and RC to Los Angeles. He talked them into dropping Milt Garrett, which they agreed to do, and eventually Lauderdale began to edge out McKee. That caused tensions. McKee and Garrett accused Charles of disloyalty, which made him angry. At the same time, he would never forfeit his budding career in the name of friendship. They returned to Seattle, where they continued to play together, but their trust in each other was broken.

Charles and Louise were fighting more as well, and when Louise's mother called, Charles told her to send her daughter a ticket if she wanted her home so bad. She did, and Louise packed to go. Both cried their hearts out. Neither knew then that she was pregnant. Lydon wrote, "Something romantic had died in Ray with the end of his first great love affair .... No other woman after Louise ever captured his whole heart and soul." Charles went into a deep depression that was similar to the one he experienced when his mother died. His drug use increased, and he began to scratch himself, a side effect of the heroin.

Lauderdale got in touch with Charles again and offered to set him up with a band in Los Angeles. Charles took off, saying good-bye to no one. McKee had been worried about the drug use going on, fearful that the police might show up and arrest them all, when he had done nothing wrong. He admitted later that it had finally been a relief when Charles left. RC Robinson no longer existed, but Ray Charles was on his way.

4

Breakthrough

In 1950, Los Angeles, California, had a population of 4 million people, 216,000 of them black. The city was second in size to New York, and it was booming. Lauderdale, who had dubbed Charles the "blind piano sensation," took him to all the hot spots. Charles took quickly to the fame game, oozing charm wherever he went. He began to move with the fast crowd; he was fascinated by women and addicted to heroin.

There was a new freedom in his music, as well. In a song he recorded in 1950, "I'll Do Anything But Work," he laughed out loud. For a few seconds, his natural voice, which had been suppressed in his efforts to sound like Nat "King" Cole, emerged and sounded, according to Lydon, "animated and innocently self-delighted." It was also obvious that 20-year-old Charles was acting as leader of the musicians who played with him, a natural role for him, when they started recording at the Universal Recording studio on Hollywood Boulevard.

BLACK MUSIC IN THE 1950s

Black music in 1950 was a subculture from which very few musicians were known to white people. Nothing was known of the record companies, disc jockeys (DJs), agents, and others who got the artists to the clubs and the records to the jukeboxes. At the same time, small record companies—independents—were beginning to sprout up all over the country. Some were started by the musicians, others by people who loved the music. Jack Lauderdale, who discovered Charles, had started as a record distributor, responsible for getting the records to the jukeboxes, and had gone on to own a small company called Down Beat, later changed to Swing Time. Like all the others, all he could hope for was a hit.

Many predicted that black music was on the cusp of something big. From 1947 to 1957, television was so popular that radio stations were forced to an all-music format in order to draw large audiences. Whites first heard black music on radio, and white teenagers especially liked it.

Radio stations pioneered the use of recorded music. Previously, radio programming had consisted mostly of talk programming, especially dramatic and comedic plays. When music came to dominate the airwaves, the key to selling records was to convince DJs on one or two leading stations in the regional market to play a certain record often. Word would spread, and, if the producers were lucky, the song would become a national hit.

In 1951, Charles was signed to Shaw Artists as part of a blues band, led by Lowell Fulson, with which he had been touring. Shaw Artists was a new agency, run by William "Billy" Shaw, who had been in the black music business for decades. It was impressive that Charles had a New York agent and an L.A. label in 1951, but to Charles, New York seemed a million miles away.

Touring became a way of life for the next two years, with some time off to record. The band boarded a bus and trav-

Charles signed with Shaw Artists as a member of Lowell Fulson's band in 1951. Fulson (above) was a blues guitarist and singer who had several hits from the 1940s to the 1970s. He was inducted into the Rock and Roll Hall of Fame in 1993.

eled from coast to coast, in the style of many groups today. They were in a world all their own, talking, throwing dice, telling jokes, playing jokes on each other, and squabbling. They became like a family. Often they would bump into other musicians they knew. Charles's good friend Quincy Jones was playing trumpet with Lionel Hampton and His Band, and they crossed paths from time to time.

In each town, Jeff Brown, the bus driver, would head to the black section, where either a black or a Jewish owner of a boardinghouse or hotel offered rooms. They grew accustomed to colored restrooms and water fountains and would stop to relieve themselves by the side of the road. They bought take-out food, which they would pick up at the back doors of restaurants.

Charles and Brown formed a friendship over time. Brown learned to step in and correct whatever mistakes Charles was making because of his blindness, either sorting out money problems or keeping Charles's clothes neat. Brown said of his friend, "Things hadn't come easy for Ray. It was a constant challenge to him to come out on top in any situation. He succeeded in music because music was his gift, but he worked on his music."

The band traveled to Cleveland and played at the Ebony Lounge. During a prior visit, Charles had met a beautician named Eileen Williams through a friend. He asked her to travel with him to Atlanta, and within a short time they decided to get married.

Charles remained with the Lowell Fulson Orchestra, stepping into the role of the chief musician. This was bound to cause some tension. Charles had transformed the group into an R&B show band, and, as they continued the tour, he wanted everything done his way. He kept demanding raises and receiving them. When the band ended its tour in L.A., he went out and bought an Oldsmobile, claiming that he was tired of the bus.

Charles recorded a song called "Baby, Let Me Hold Your Hand" during this time, and it put him back on the charts for a short time. This song was instrumental in establishing him in the record industry, but it troubled him that people continued to tell him that he sounded like another singer, Charles Brown. He began to realize that he wanted people to compliment him for sounding like himself, not like someone else. He needed to find his own voice.

Jack Lauderdale, in the meantime, was heading into bankruptcy because of a lack of big hits. He did not think that

Charles had been sensational enough and decided to put his contract up for sale, similar to the way in which baseball players are traded today. He kept Lowell Fulson, however.

ATLANTIC RECORDS

Herb Abramson and Ahmet Ertegun had formed a record company, Atlantic Records, and were seeking talent. They agreed to purchase Ray Charles's contract for the price of $2,500. Just like that, Charles became an Atlantic recording artist. By luck, the Lowell Fulson Orchestra had been booked on the Northeast theater circuit, which covered Baltimore, Philadelphia, Washington, D.C., New York, and other cities. Charles made his debut at the Apollo Theater, the famous Harlem venue on 125th Street, and soon met Abramson, who had bought his contract. He also met Billy Shaw, his agent, who told him in no uncertain terms that, if he didn't make money for them, they would let him go. Charles didn't mind the straight talk, but the warning put a lot of pressure on him.

It was on to Chicago after that, where the final argument occurred between Charles and Lowell Fulson. Charles felt betrayed by Fulson when he realized that Shaw Artists was paying Fulson a higher price for Charles than Charles was receiving. Fulson pocketed the money that made up the difference, which was standard practice at the time. Charles quit the tour. Fulson said good-bye with no hard feelings, but Charles simmered for years over the betrayal he felt.

When Charles got home, he realized that Eileen had been drinking on a regular basis, a habit he would not tolerate in a woman. He ended the marriage. He tried to get someone else to buy his contract from Atlantic but was turned down. He was despondent about these events in his life, but, as he had done in the past, he got back to work. It was time to record for Atlantic Records.

Charles's frustration was increasing; he worried that he might never get a big band going. He went to the office of Atlantic Records in September after playing at the Apollo

Theater in Harlem and started to record. The songs generally were imitative of other singers like Nat "King" Cole, but the fourth song on the record, "The Sun's Gonna Shine Again," was unlike anything the producers had ever heard. Still, they decided to be safe and choose the imitative numbers. The record did not take off. Ertegun finally figured out the reason for that: Their New York musicians didn't get the blues side of Charles. They weren't from the South.

Atlantic released a second single from Charles's September session and kept hoping that there would be a breakthrough. *Billboard* gave the song "Mess Around" a rave, which made Atlantic executives hopeful. Ertegun had a gut feeling that Charles was going to find his true voice and soar, which Atlantic needed. It was still a new company, and everything hinged on finding a hit. At that time, four major record companies— Columbia, RCA Victor, Decca, and Capitol—dominated the industry. They sold 85 percent of the 200 million records that Americans bought in 1950.

FINDING HIS OWN VOICE

Charles knew that his music was growing more powerful, but he had not had a chance to prove it. "I was trying to get a pulse," he said, "Slowly I began to wean myself [from imitation] and come into my own, but was not about to give up what I already had."

A musician named Eddie Lee Jones of Greenwood, Mississippi, who called himself Guitar Slim, helped to turn Charles around. Slim had the courage to reach for the joys and the musical possibilities. More important, he had no qualms about shameless self-expression.

During Charles's second recording session for Atlantic, Ertegun was determined to find Charles's true sound. They took their time, with Charles playing whatever he felt like. Relaxed, he chatted with Ertegun. As the rehearsal geared up, the initial tension between the control room and Charles eased, and at one point Ertegun even joined him in a song. A week later, they were back in the studio. Jesse Stone, a band leader, songwriter, and music arranger, was brought in to arrange the new tracks.

The work was paying off, and Charles was on a roll. Then a telephone call interrupted the session. Someone was calling to report the death of Mary Jane Robinson, who had been like a second mother to Charles. Tom Dowd, the recording engineer, entered the studio and announced the news to Charles.

Charles knew she was sick and had been paying her medical bills, but Robinson's death was a shock nevertheless. He was completely still for a few moments, while everyone held their breath. Finally, Charles told them to continue. The session that followed was Charles's best to date. It was a magical time: Stone's arrangements blended with the moods of each

A Complex Character

Ray Charles was scarred from boyhood. He became addicted to heroin at the age of 17 and was also addicted to alcohol, women, and work. The addictions made him unpredictable; one moment, he could be charming and laughing and the next he was cold and fierce.

Michael Lydon wrote about the drug that was so important to Ray for more than 16 years: "Heroin became a private pleasure for which Charles paid a high price in money, time wasted, and opportunities lost. Heroin humiliated Ray Charles and nearly killed him; the lies and secrets attendant on addiction scarred his character with a sour mistrust of other people."

His public persona was spellbinding, warm, and affable, but those close to him had to put up with a temperamental master. He had an obsessive need to be in control. He was wary of strangers and was described by many as stand-offish. His musical manager, Renald Richard said, "With Ray, if you do him wrong, he'll hug you, smile at you, pretend that you're still his best friend, but inside he's thinking, 'You did me wrong, and I'm gonna slice you for it.' And he will get back at you somehow." During his lifetime, he was accused of being selfish, narcissistic, and downright mean, yet he is also remembered for his self-confidence, his huge sense of responsibility to numerous people, and his humor.

David Hoffman, Charles's trumpet soloist arranger for many years, said of his boss, "He is a legend and an icon. There were ups and downs working song and Charles sang with a new freedom, the sound of his voice ranging from agony to cheerfulness. Ertegun was thrilled with the recording. After they were done, Charles went back to Greenville to bury Robinson. He was 22.

At that session was a man named Jerry Wexler, who had just become a partner at Atlantic Records after investing $2,000. One of his first experiences as a fledgling producer was to sit back and watch Ray Charles work. The session left him in awe.

MEETING DELLA

Della Beatrice Howard was a plump woman around Charles's age who had a radiant smile and cheerful disposition. She sang with the Cecil Shaw Singers, and while in Houston she heard

for Ray. He could be decidedly unpleasant at times, and extremely self-centered. He has forgotten the people that enabled his success, much like many in his position."

The women who were close to him ended up wondering if he had ever loved anyone. Ruth Robinson, who knew Charles for many years, said, "It's possible that he loved each of us or some of us or none of us. I don't know. I *thought* that he loved me, I believed it for a long time. And I still don't know that it's *not* true." Both she and Susaye Green found Charles great fun to be with. Green was close enough to him to see that his feelings were easily hurt and that his spirit was sad a lot. It was clear to both women that the scars from his childhood were never healed and that he saw his life as a lonely battle. Green said, "There's a piece missing in his heart that he fills with music, not with other human beings. He put up walls to keep people out, didn't share his real feelings with anyone." Both came to feel betrayed by him.

Charles was never able to rid himself of the demons that plagued him. Music was the driving force in his life. Everything and everyone in his life was there to make the music happen. It was his solace and his salvation, and it contained what everyone close to him seemed to be seeking but could not find: tenderness, love, longing, joy, and redemption. In the end, it was his audiences who were most blessed by Ray Charles.

Charles being interviewed on the radio. He talked about how he loved gospel singing and that one of his favorite groups was the Cecil Shaw Singers. Howard called the station and offered to introduce Charles to Cecil Shaw.

Howard had been singing and touring with Shaw since she graduated from high school. It was known that gospel singers worked as hard as R&B singers, and Charles was drawn instantly to Howard's down-to-earth qualities. After he went back on the road, he called her often and wrote love letters to her on a portable typewriter. He wanted her to move to Dallas with him, so they could start fresh. He thought Houston was too humid and more racist than Dallas.

In the meantime, Ertegun and partner Jerry Wexler went south again to meet up with Charles and to listen to the original songs he was arranging. His growth was obvious. The musical elements he had come to know well—big band jazz, deep blues, and fervid gospel—were merging. The sound was distinctly Ray Charles.

He later explained the lyrics to his songs to Joe Goldberg, author of *Jazz Masters of the Fifties*:

> The things I write and sing about concern the general Joe and his general problems. There are four basic things: love, somebody runnin' his mouth too much, having fun, and jobs are hard to get.... When I put myself in the place of the ... general Joe I'm singing about ... I sing with all the feeling I can put into it, so that I can feel it myself.

On December 31, he rang in the New Year by playing the Sam Houston Coliseum, the fourth year he had done so. He hoped that 1954 would be different.

THE BREAKTHROUGH SONG

Charles's songs "The Things I Used to Do" and "It Should Have Been Me" were climbing the R&B charts. Charles was also using drugs more frequently. Heroin had always made him itch, and when high he would flail his arms and legs and scratch. He would also become extreme in temperament, being either manic or very low. He now had someone to get high with—new saxophonist David "Fathead" Newman. It was unsettling for the other band member, Renald Richard. According to Lydon, as drug users are prone to do, Newman and Charles made their habit a "cool secret language that squares . . . would never understand." Richard, the new musical director, was a square and did not approve of the drugs.

One night the band was rolling along on the highway, when Charles started to sing along to a gospel tune. He sang, "I got a woman," and Richard said, "Yeah, she lives across town," then Charles responded, "She's good to me." Charles asked Richard to write it up. "I Got a Woman" fused the blues and gospel sounds together, creating a new sound called "soul." Charles liked it immediately, and, after playing it in a few clubs, he knew he had something. He called Wexler and Ertegun, and they flew to Atlanta for a show, as Charles had added three other songs. When Ertegun and Wexler entered the club where the band was playing, the band leapt into "I Got a Woman." Charles kept on, playing a succession of new songs. Both men were stunned by the brilliance of the new work. Wexler said, "I knew something fantastic had happened." They had to record immediately. Wexler said what they were all thinking: Charles was ready for fame. The song took cities like Durham, Atlanta, and Nashville by storm, and quickly reached number one on the R&B chart.

5

Song by Song

Rock and roll took off in 1955. Parents hated it: They found it disturbing and frenzied, and, along with the clergy, they began to blame the music for the youthful rebellion that was taking place. Some towns even banned the music. Teens, on the other hand, were enthralled with rock and roll. The singers who were creating lyrics about the joys and agonies of adolescence had great appeal to their young listeners. There was so much music being produced that *Billboard* eventually began to list the top 100 records.

The 1950s were the beginning of a consumer culture, as Americans, including teens, became more prosperous. They bought rock and roll records and transistor radios and watched *American Bandstand* on television. Many radio stations across the country were playing black music, fed by the small, independent record companies who brought regional groups into the national record market. Alan Freed, a DJ for radio station

WJW in Cleveland, Ohio, was one of the first to promote the new music nationally; he coined the term "rock and roll."

Writing for *Historical Text Archives*, Donald J. Mabry said, "Had parents not indulged their children with money, the rock 'n' roll revolution would never have occurred." This was the first time in history that teenagers were such a force in history. Mabry wrote, "The teenagers of the 1950's desegregated popular music, but not consciously. They just liked the sounds." Teens were listening to all kinds of sounds, including "The Chipmunk Song" by Alvin and the Chipmunks and "Sugartime" by the McGuire Sisters. In 1955, Charles's "I Got a Woman" was the R&B DJs' ninth-most-played record, and Charles was the seventh-favorite artist. This was a tremendous leap forward.

AN UNUSUAL LIFESTYLE

Della Howard and Ray Charles were married in Dallas. As much as Charles claimed that he wanted a home life and a family, life on the road, with women and drugs, was too ingrained in him. In addition, nothing was going to stop his rise to fame. He began to divide his life into two compartments, the family man and the road musician, and he made sure that one did not bump up against the other. In May, Della gave birth to a son. They named him Ray Charles Robinson Jr.

Charles was back on the road within days. A woman named Mary Ann Fisher, who was singing blues at the Orchid Club in Louisville, Kentucky, auditioned for Charles. He told her that he would be back through in a month; if she wanted to join his band, she could come on then as a featured vocalist. There was little for her to think about; of course she would join.

With his "wild man" style, Guitar Slim, who had had such a big influence on Charles, had become a role model for many musicians entering the field. Charles began to take charge of his music. He stood up to Wexler and Ertegun when he was feeling pushed during a session, declaring that he would do it his way or not at all. The two producers agreed to step back.

Ray Charles holds hands with his wife, Della Howard Robinson, in front of their home. Also with them are their three sons: David, Ray Charles Jr. (in striped shirt), and Robert (front).

At this time, Charles was learning to use his emotions in his music to make art. He still went from bass to a high pitch, but his music was subtler, more tender. By opening himself, he was opening the souls of his listeners. One song Charles recorded, "A Fool for You," had Ertegun and Wexler declaring that it was the best record they had ever made.

Charles and his band had gone up in status, they realized, when they were billed above Lowell Fulson in Atlanta. The band went on to Dayton, Ohio, and picked up Mary Ann Fisher. She fell in love with Charles, who nicknamed her "Fish." Her life had been hard, but she was fun. One of the band members called her "a black Mae West." (West was a white actress and playwright who was popular from the 1920s to the 1940s.)

Jeff Brown and Ray Charles were by now close friends, and Brown was put in charge of paying band members and keeping them on time, but he was not given a raise. Charles had a reputation for being cheap with the band members, and he cut individual deals with each of them, which created a lot of jealousy. They always had to deal with Brown when it came to money, but they knew that the orders came from Charles.

Brown was one of the first to notice Charles's coldness, that he wasn't friendly with anyone in the band and made an effort to remain detached from people. He said that Charles liked people to the extent that they could do something for him. Still, Charles's character flaws did not drive Brown away—not then, anyway.

BUSTED AGAIN

Throughout this time, drugs were a constant problem. In the summer of 1955, Brown accompanied one band member to a doctor's office, but the physician made them leave because the musician was high on drugs. In November 1955, the band entered Philadelphia, a city on edge about drugs. The police raids seemed to target black users in particular.

In Philadelphia, Charles and his band were appearing at the Town Hall Ballroom. He and three band members locked the door of their dressing room to get high, and when they heard loud pounding on the door, they ignored it. A popular DJ named Kae Williams had suspected that the band was using drugs and called the police. Charles and the others were arrested. They, along with the five who were innocent, were taken to headquarters, fingerprinted, and kept overnight. All nine were held on $2,000 bail, and the story appeared on the front page of the Philadelphia *Tribune*. In the end, Charles agreed to pay $6,000 to wipe the slate clean, and it took a week for him to get everyone out. The arrest did not affect Charles much, but the publicity around his heroin use did, as it became public knowledge that he had an addiction. Everyone, though, including Wexler and Ertegun, kept a hands-off attitude.

A STEADY RISE TO THE TOP

Charles was ready to get on with the recording of his new songs and wanted a female vocal group to back him up. Someone suggested a group called the Cookies. These three teenage girls were led by a raspy-voiced singer, Margie Hendricks. With the Cookies, Charles recorded the songs "Hallelujah I Love Her So," "Mary Ann," and "What Would I Do Without You," all original, and he added to that a song that he had already recorded, "Drown in My Own Tears." Once again, Ertegun and Wexler were thrilled. Ertegun said, "Ray developed an uncanny feel for structuring a song to grab the audience." After receiving ecstatic reviews in a magazine called *Down Beat*, Charles tried to explain his motive for making the music he did: "I try to bring out my soul so that people can understand what I am. I want people to feel my soul."

Nat "King" Cole, Count Basie, Ella Fitzgerald, and Louis Armstrong were topping the black national lists, along with rock and roll singers Chuck Berry, Fats Domino, and the Platters. After "I Got a Woman" was released, Charles's name was appearing among those of jazz greats Ruth Brown, Muddy Waters, and the Moonglows.

Charles's life over the next few years was filled with constant touring, writing songs, and checking in on his family. He recorded an average of three singles each year. Della Robinson gave birth to another son, and Charles moved the family to Los Angeles. In 1956, Elvis Presley recorded Charles's song "I Got a Woman," which augmented its popularity among whites, as well as increasing Charles's income. It was obvious to all that the barriers between white music and black music were slowly disappearing. Still, while Elvis and other white artists made records that went to the top of the pop, country and western, and R&B charts, blacks were lucky to get onto the white charts at all. It was a one-way street.

BECOMING A BUSINESSMAN

Charles's music was more adult than Elvis's—its content harder for teens to relate to—which was one reason producers thought white teens were not buying the records. At this point, Charles took a giant step into jazz, recording an album with Ahmet Ertegun's brother, Nesuhi. It was brilliant. Charles immediately followed it with another R&B album. He used the back-up voices of the Cookies more to create a new sound. He wanted to take Margie Hendricks, Ethel McRae, and Dorothy Jones on the road, but he did not think he could afford it.

Two big changes occurred in Charles's musical career at this time: Atlantic Records moved to a bigger space on West 57th Street, and his agent, Billy Shaw, dropped dead of a heart attack. The latter event was a shock, but business carried on with Shaw's son, Milt. Renald Richard was back touring with Charles, and he noticed immediately that heroin was still a big problem with the band, and that band members often squabbled with Charles. Mary Ann Fisher, too, had come to hate heroin. Charles tried to get her to join him when he used, but she refused. Once, he hit her so hard that she was hospitalized for three days. Another time, when the band members

IN HIS OWN WORDS...

If all artists would do what is really right for them and would feel within themselves what they are doing, they would stay up there longer. A new star is born every day, but it's always a question of how long he will shine. A true artist will be around for a long time.

Quoted in Michael Lydon, *Ray Charles: Man and Music.* New York: Routledge, 2004.

ran out of drugs, Charles talked Fisher into flying to New York to secure more. She was terrified, but she did it. Nonetheless, Fisher was starting to feel worn down by the women who surrounded Charles and the drug use, which was often accompanied by violence.

Meanwhile, Charles's music kept evolving. The licensing company, Broadcast Music, Inc. (BMI), sent Charles and Richard steady checks for "I Got a Woman." Atlantic, in contrast, was charging inflated fees for recording expenses and other services, like other record companies did. This annoyed Charles, but he knew that it was common practice. It made him think, though, about what it would be like to be his own producer even though he knew those days were far off. He kept expenses low, often by not paying his musicians enough, and his accountant kept the books up to date and taxes paid. When the cash came in, Charles deposited it in various banks

Atlantic Records

Herb Abramson and Ahmet Ertegun, founders of Atlantic Records, could not have been more opposite. Michael Lydon, Charles's biographer, said that "Abramson was a dynamic Jew and Ertegun a bald Turk who liked to talk." What brought them together was a love of jazz. Ahmet Ertegun and his brother, Nesuhi, fell in love with jazz when they heard Duke Ellington in London in 1933, and the love only grew when their father became the Turkish ambassador to the United States during World War II. After their father died, Ertegun studied international law at Georgetown University with the plan to follow in his father's footsteps. Black music won over law, however, and Ertegun went to New York to make records. He and Abramson, who had been trained as a dentist, had met earlier. Herb and his wife, Miriam, had already created a plan for a record company, but they did not know where to go for money. The three banded together and pooled their resources. The Abramsons and Ertegun put in $2,500 each, and they borrowed $10,000 from Ertegun's family dentist. They became the proud owners of Atlantic Records.

Pop fans would come to recognize the "Atlantic sound," a funky elegance that blended the diverse tastes of the owners. The Abramsons wanted to jump in New York after sending some to his wife. The Greenville bank account also stayed active. Charles's finances eventually became strong enough that the Shaws of Shaw Artists borrowed from him.

Charles was immensely talented in jazz and pop, but he had not yet found a way to combine his knowledge and talent into music that would appeal to a larger audience. He and Quincy Jones started to put together a jazz album, with Jones writing six songs and Charles contributing others. The next day, the same band recorded four R&B sides. Charles was unstoppable. The song "It's All Right" created a new connection between Charles and the Cookies, whose voices reach out to him as he sings, "So many times I sit down to cry."

Ertegun and Wexler had to decide how to produce the album for all the new songs. They did something highly unusual at the time: They launched an R&B singles artist as a jazz album

right into contemporary R&B. All three took it seriously, going down south to Atlanta and New Orleans to see what was happening.

When Ertegun heard Ray Charles sing "Baby, Let Me Hold Your Hand" in 1949 or 1950, he thought Charles was the most fabulous singer alive. When the group took Charles on, Ertegun was the only one who was sure that Charles could make a hit song. They brought a man named Jerry Wexler on board when Abramson was called back into the service. Wexler had coined the phrase *rhythm and blues* in an article he wrote for the *Saturday Review of Literature*.

The Atlantic owners were devastated when Charles decided to go with ABC-Paramount in 1960. They had nurtured him to the top, song by song, and now he was betraying them.

Wexler and Ertegun became a famous team, recording Aretha Franklin, the Rolling Stones, Bette Midler, the Bee Gees, the Allman Brothers, and Phil Collins, to name a few. It was perhaps poetic justice that Charles came crawling back to them in 1977, when everyone else had abandoned him. They welcomed him back into the fold.

Ahmet Ertegun, one of two cofounders of Atlantic Records, was born in Istanbul, Turkey. At age 13, he moved with his family to the United States. In 1947, Ertegun and his business partner, Herb Abramson, formed the recording company that would make Ray Charles a star. Ertegun is shown here in his office at Atlantic in 2005. He died in December 2006.

artist. Their timing was uncanny, though, for a change was occurring in listeners across the country. They were turning to jazz and focusing more on sound than on lyrics.

LIFE ON THE ROAD

With all the work and the produced albums, Charles felt like he was in a slump. The music, according to Lydon, had a "sweaty, funky flavor," but in truth, Ray Charles and His Orchestra were still just another band playing four or five nights out of the week in tobacco warehouses and all kinds of joints. The audiences were rough, and it was not uncommon for fights to break out. After two years on the road, some of the band members wanted out, and others left because Charles was looking for better talent.

Thirteen bodies jammed the two cars Charles took on the road, as he was finally able to bring the Cookies on tour. After Dorothy Jones quit, Margie Hendricks brought on a 16-year-old girl, Mae Mosely Lyles. Charles had to get permission from her mother, who was only five years older than Charles himself, for her daughter to join them.

The girls on tour were constantly battling for Charles's attention, and he played one Cookie against the other, often turning to one while cold-shouldering another. Jeff Brown's wife, Sheila, said, "Ray could be a mean and selfish man. . . . If you didn't know how to stand up for yourself, he'd try to control you. He had no use for any girl he couldn't get on drugs."

Charles had songs titled "Mary Ann" and "Margie." Each girl felt as though she was "the one" when he sang her song. Charles's main girl of the moment was awarded a seat in his Cadillac, and when Mary Ann Fisher was replaced by Hendricks, there were hard feelings. Hendricks would use drugs with Charles, though, which gave her an advantage. Charles also loved her voice: Their voices resonated together, creating a special magic. Charles had a growly voice that exploded like a gospel singer. With all the drama taking place, the girls knew that, if they got out of line, they would be shipped out, so they were careful. It didn't help when another girl came on board in September 1956. Her name was Gwen Berry, and she was nicknamed "Squat" because she was so short. In the meantime, Della Robinson was expecting another baby.

A NEW RECORDING SYSTEM

Tom Dowd at Atlantic Records was in charge of mastering the tapes of Charles's sessions (*mastering* means "taking the goofs out"). Dowd had a screw-arm lathe and a turntable. According to Michael Lydon, "An aluminum disc coated with cellulose nitrate sat on the turntable; a cutting head hung from the lathe." Dowd would play the edited tapes and set the disc spinning, "vibrating a sapphire needle held between them." The needle cut a spiral groove in the cellulose, turning the music into wiggles in the groove. This became the master. The master went to a pressing plant in New Jersey, where it was electroplated with silver and backed with copper to keep it rigid. An intricate process followed, with the end result being the record.

In 1958, the recording process started undergoing changes. Dowd bought an eight-track recorder, which allowed many sound sources to be recorded separately, with each track so well isolated that any could be changed or rerecorded without affecting the others. While recording with his band one day, Charles heard something he didn't like with the bass. Dowd played it back for him over the studio's stereo speakers. Michael Lydon wrote, "Ray jumped up like he'd been hit by an electric shock." From then on Charles was hooked on the new technology. He became a master of the art of recording.

NEWPORT JAZZ FESTIVAL

Sixty thousand jazz buffs met in Newport, Rhode Island, in 1958 for the Newport Jazz Festival, which had been running for five years under the guidance of a promoter named George Wein. This was to be Charles's initiation into the jazz scene, and he was booked for Saturday night, "blues night." He was up against greats like Miles Davis, John Coltrane, and Duke Ellington, and he knew it. He would be performing in the same venue with Chuck Berry and others who drew a young crowd.

In the end, it was a disappointment. Two major music publications, *Down Beat* and *Billboard*, reported that Charles did not form the rapport with his audience that they had expected.

THE CROSSOVER SONG

Then came the fateful night when Charles and the orchestra were in a town called Brownsville, near Pittsburgh. Charles had run out of things to play. He told the band to follow him and turned to the ladies and told them to repeat after him. It was all improvisation after that. The audience went wild as Charles kept shouting, "What'd I say?" Fans demanding the record would have been shocked to learn that the song was made up on the spot. As the band went on to Indianapolis, the newspaper *The Recorder*, announced in an ad, "*On Same Bill, Those Gorgeous Girls, THE RAELETTES.*" The Cookies had a new name.

After that performance, Charles at last had a big band to work with. They completed six tracks in one afternoon of recording, among them the songs "Let the Good Times Roll" and "When Your Lover Has Gone." Just a few days later, Ray Charles and the Raelettes completed an album.

The single, "What'd I Say," got off to a slow start, but after Tom Dowd at Atlantic downplayed some of the parts that he thought white audiences would find too suggestive, it took off. By the time it was number 26 on the pop charts, it was blasting out of radios all over the country. It made it to number two on the R&B charts. Charles earned a lot of money in royalties and gave Atlantic its first-ever million in gross sales during a one-month period. Both the independent record company and Charles were at the top of their game. There was nowhere to go but up—or so they thought.

6

Fame

Charles's agents at Shaw Artists, Larry Myers and Milt Shaw, began to dream big. The white world was ready to open its doors to Charles, but Atlantic Records was a black label. Myers worried that, if Charles stayed with Atlantic, he would end up staying in the black world. It also was not lost on him that Charles's contract with Atlantic was running out and new negotiations were in order.

At first, Charles was opposed to the idea of switching record companies; he was happy with Atlantic Records. After all, Ertegun and Wexler had believed in him and given him the time and space to rise slowly to the top. He decided to stall contract negotiations, though, and see what happened. Ertegun and Wexler wanted a signed contract and were worried by Charles's actions. Ertegun even went out to the Midwest, contract in hand, to try to get Charles to sign, but Charles refused.

In the meantime, Myers was in action. He went to Harry Levine, who was at ABC-Paramount Records, one of the newer major recording companies. Its parent company, American Broadcasting-Paramount Theaters, was the backbone of the company. Created four years before, it was still searching for an identity. Directors there had been advised to get into rock and roll, either black or white music, but with the black sound. Who better than Ray Charles? The problem was that the directors had to entice him away from Atlantic Records, so they approached him with terms that would allow him to produce his own records. Charles would be the artist, as well as the businessman/producer. That had never been done before. Charles was ready to talk.

ABC-Paramount offered Charles a three-year contract, guaranteeing him $50,000 a year for three years. The hook, though, was that, if Charles's albums were a success, he would make 75 cents out of every dollar. Charles said that he wanted to give Ertegun and Wexler a chance to match it. Before the meeting ended, though, he came up with another idea. He told the ABC-Paramount producers that he wanted to own his own masters. According to Lydon, "Master tapes were the ultimate source of a company's value, the right to lease them for reissue a source of long-term revenue." No company was willing to let its masters go, unless they were forced to by bankruptcy. Charles was bluffing, but no one knew that. They finally came back and said that, after five years, he could own them. They added the stipulations that he had to produce 12 tracks a year. If he did not do so, the contract year would keep running until he did them all. Charles's lawyer thought that it was a fantastic deal.

Charles went back on tour. Ertegun and Wexler rushed out the album he had recorded for them called *The Genius of Ray Charles* and put a full-page ad in *Billboard* to plug his single "I'm Movin' On." They had nurtured Charles on his way to the top and could not believe that he was seriously considering leaving them. The next thing they knew, Charles had signed with ABC-Paramount. They were devastated.

Leaving Atlantic Records was a gamble for Charles, but agents Milt Shaw and Larry Myers became determined to move him into more sophisticated gigs. Charles had already started to trade in his Cadillac every year and to wear custom-made silk suits and tuxedos. In 1959, he had grossed well over $100,000.

Jeff Brown, who had worked as Charles's manager for years, did not understand the complexity of the new contracts and felt uncomfortable in lawyers' offices. Charles was clear that Brown would not get anything from record profits, for he was still an employee, but he did list Brown as a minority owner of the new record company he was forming under ABC, called Tangerine, named after his favorite fruit.

The first ABC session was weak, and in fact the producers hated it. They were obligated by their contract to release it, however, so they pressed 5,000 copies. Almost none sold. In the meantime, Atlantic Records released a single of "Let the Good Times Roll" and it hit the pop charts.

In 1960, a man named Hal Zeiger began to promote and book sell-out shows for Charles. Charles was determined to create a big seller for ABC, and he came up with the idea of singing songs with place names, songs like "Georgia on My Mind" and "Carry Me Back to Old Virginny." The producers loved the album and called it *Genius Hits the Road*.

Things were picking up. Charles was a hit at the Newport Jazz Festival that year, creating a frenzy with "What'd I Say." He bought a bus to use for touring and invested in an airplane—the latter had been a dream since a fan had introduced him to a private plane. Flying in his new five-passenger Cessna 310 thrilled Charles, and before long he learned all about its mechanics.

Charles recorded another album for ABC called *Dedicated to You*, a group of romantic songs. At this time, he was making polished albums in pop mode, but most of the songs did not have the raw feelings that fans had come to associate with him. Onstage, however, he remained "the genius."

French reporter Frank Tenot wrote about Charles after seeing him perform:

> Behind a tiny electric piano that sounds like a guitar at times, sat Ray Charles. His dead eyes and his temples are hidden by enormous glasses which are almost a mask. He's dressed in a sumptuous tuxedo with silk lapels. He sways from right to left, smiles, grimaces rather, moves his legs under him and, keeping the music going without losing tempo, he adjusts the volume of his voice and his instrument with an amplifier next to his piano.

"Georgia on My Mind" reached number one on the Billboard chart in November 1960. The ballad about the yearning for home had huge nostalgic appeal for listeners. The producers at ABC were ecstatic.

The National Association of Recording Arts and Sciences presented Charles with four Grammy Awards that year: best performance by a pop single artist and best vocal performance single record or track, male ("Georgia on My Mind"); best vocal performance album (*The Genius of Ray Charles*); and best R&B performance ("Let the Good Times Roll"). Charles was happy, but as always, he did not bask in the limelight for long. He was immediately on to the next project. That year, he earned $800,000.

WOMEN AND DRUGS

Charles's romantic life was similarly frenetic. Though he was married, he had many girlfriends outside of the marriage. Charles was discreet and yet open about all the women in his life. At the peak of his success, he learned that one of his girlfriends, Mae Mosely Lyles, was going to have a baby, as was his wife.

When Charles missed a couple of concerts, the members of his inner circle knew what was going on: Heroin was beginning to affect his career. Still, the tour continued across the country. On a show called *Kraft Music Hall,* Charles's television debut, he acted nervous and withdrawn, and the general conclusion was that his debut was a dud.

Charles spent March 1961 at home in Los Angeles, using heroin regularly. One day his son Ray Jr. sneaked into his dad's room against his mother's orders. He found Charles on the floor, covered in blood. He had fallen and sliced his left hand with glass, severing an artery. The doctor told Charles that he could not play for six weeks, but he would have none of it. He continued the tour, playing with one hand.

In Detroit, a blind teenage boy called Little Stevie Wonder performed on stage with Charles, his idol. During this time in Detroit—spring of 1961—Charles met Joe Adams, who would spend the rest of his life by Charles's side.

Zeiger wanted Charles to have a master of ceremonies for his shows, someone black and sophisticated. Adams was involved in many aspects of radio and had been a successful character actor in numerous films, as well as an actor on Broadway. Immediately, he noticed that the lighting for Charles's shows was all wrong, and he jumped in to fix it. Charles was impressed with the tall, sophisticated man who had been successful on his own and offered him a job.

It was a busy year: Charles had won the Grammy awards, five of his albums were on the LP chart, and his wife gave birth to a third son. The band's tour ended at Carnegie Hall in New York, after which Charles and the band headed back to L.A.

Once he was back in Los Angeles, Charles ran into an old buddy, Percy Mayfield. Mayfield had written a song called "Hit the Road Jack" that he thought would work well for the Raelettes. He also had a song called "Danger Zone." Charles liked both. He requested another song, one about "a woman you do the best you can for, but on the other hand. . . ." Mayfield agreed. At an impromptu recording session shortly after, Charles sang the song he had requested, "But on the Other Hand, Baby" and then went right into "Hit the Road Jack." The ABC producers knew they had another hit with the second record. The song, which depicts a couple fighting, was funny, and people could dance to it. The following week, 8,000 fans crowded into a hall designed for 5,000 in New Jersey. They could not get enough of Ray Charles.

Along with the fame came a bigger drive for heroin. One time when Charles was at a dealer's house buying heroin, the police busted him. Charles tried hiding the heroin under his dental bridge but he was still taken to the police station. Jeff Brown rushed down to the jail and got him out. The case was dismissed because the judge ruled it an illegal search, but it was a close call.

GOING ABROAD

Charles and the Raelettes next headed to the south of France to perform at the Juan-les-Pins International Jazz Festival. It was the first time any of them had been to Europe, including 16-year-old Mae Lyles, who was traveling with Charles for this gig.

He was still on heroin, and it was becoming obvious. At one press conference, a photographer made the cameraman stop filming when Charles started to scratch himself so intensely

IN HIS OWN WORDS...

I've met many of my early goals: I've played Carnegie Hall. I've got a big band. I've some Grammys, though I forget when and for what. But I never dreamed when I started out that I'd become known in two-thirds of the world. If you had told me in 1952 that one day I'd be flying to Singapore and Sydney for gigs, I'd have said, "Baby, I may be blind, but I ain't dumb; I'll be lucky to keep working the chitlin circuit [Southern slang for low-class bars]."

Ray Charles and David Ritz, *Brother Ray: Ray Charles' Own Story*. New York: Da Capo Press, 1978 that it was embarrassing. The show was a huge success, however, and they traveled to Zurich, Lyons, and Paris. The booker wanted them back as soon as possible.

The band then flew back to the United States to do a show in Memphis, Tennessee. The year before, Charles had announced that he was not going to play to segregated audiences anymore, and he stuck to his guns. The black promoter in Memphis decided to take a risk and booked an integrated show. To everyone's amazement, nothing happened. Blacks and whites danced side by side.

Back in New York, Mae Lyles gave birth to a baby girl she named Raenee, who was born with congenital glaucoma. Charles offered to pay all medical expenses and for a full-time nurse. There was no time to visit the baby, though, as he was preparing for a concert at the Hollywood Bowl. Charles went all out for the show: He had a 15-piece band, a 19-piece string section, and a 12-voice chorus by this time. The audience— 6,000 people—went wild.

Charles and his band went straight back to Europe. A photograph in *Jazz* magazine showed Charles on the balcony of an elegant Paris hotel, with the Arc de Triomphe behind him. He had captivated the residents of Paris to a degree that reporters found difficult to describe. Charles told journalists that "the blues was the greatest expression of Negro music," and Frank Tenot thought that Charles had brought "modern R&B to France." The tour was a huge success. Charles was 31 years old and at the top of his game.

FALL FROM GRACE

Charles and the band returned to the United States and immediately started another tour. Backstage at a gig in Indianapolis, Charles heard a knock at the door. He opened it and found himself face to face with two police detectives, who rushed in and searched the room. They found a lot of drugs and arrested Charles. He was charged with a violation of the

Ray Charles was arrested for possession of heroin in 1961. It was his second arrest for drug possession; he would be arrested a third time in 1964. Here, Indianapolis detectives interview Charles at the police station in 1961.

1935 narcotics act and with being a common drug addict. No one had ever seen Charles lose control, but that day he began to cry softly and then to sob. The police let reporters interview their prisoner, and Charles told them that he had started using at age 16. He indulged in a bout of self-pity and blamed the addiction on the circumstances of his life. He got out on bail and covered his head with his coat as he left the police station. He had a concert scheduled miles away that he was allowed to go to, but once backstage he was still agitated, to the point of jumping up and down uncontrollably. Then he began to deny everything he had said earlier.

News of the arrest spread across the nation, and reporters and television cameras jammed the halls outside the courtroom at Charles's sentencing. Charles was released on a $1,000 bond. Ed Sullivan postponed Charles's appearance on his television show, but Charles went on to a sold-out gig in Nashville, where a full audience cheered him on. Still, promoters were nervous. Could they be guaranteed that he would show up? Additional appearances were canceled, and the press wrote about the bust for three months.

It had been a traumatic experience for Charles. Afterwards, detectives across the country kept a close watch on him, often showing up backstage for no reason. The police were relentless, always checking in. As much as the cops wanted to arrest him, though, they also loved him. Charles, in turn, was learning to

Ray and Elvis

In November 1960, *Billboard*'s headline read, "Ray Charles and Elvis Hit with Sweet Stuff: two pioneers of the rock 'n roll school are bigger than ever on Billboard's Hot 100, and they're doing it with ballads." Charles's was "Georgia on My Mind" and Elvis's was "Are You Lonesome Tonight?"

Elvis Presley made his debut in 1956. His manager, Sam Phillips, had said before discovering Presley, "If I could find a white who had the Negro feel, I could make a million dollars." Presley fit the bill.

At an audition at a recording studio in Memphis, Presley was asked what his style was. He replied, "I don't sound like nobody." Presley was at the beginning of the new music that was, said *New York Times* writer Peter Guralnick, "rich with Negro and hillbilly lore"—rock 'n roll. Presley had been considered a hillbilly singer until his record "That's All Right, Mama" was released. He was combining country with rhythm and blues, following in the footsteps of Ray Charles and other black singers.

Some people in the white community thought that Presley was trying to put down pop music and bring in black music. Curiously, there wasn't much backlash from blacks, perhaps because, when Presley sang their songs, it somehow made them more respectable to the white world and brought in more money for them. Also, Presley gave credit where credit was due. Once fight the law with money. "Just like you can buy grades of silk, you can buy grades of law," he was quoted as saying. Charles bought his for $6,000. An Indianapolis lawyer defended him, saying that the police had entered Charles's room without a warrant.

Charles's stubbornness came out, and he claimed that no one was going to tell him what he could put in his body. He clung to his drug habit, even though the drugs were affecting his body in noticeable ways. He wiggled and twitched and slapped himself constantly.

ON A ROLL

Despite his personal problems, it seemed that Charles could not go wrong with his music in 1962. He decided to do a

he said, "I can't sing 'Ain't That a Shame' like Fats Domino. I know that." In the early years of rock and roll, Presley was seen as something of a hero. Black singer Little Richard summed up his take on Presley when he said, "Thank God for Elvis Presley."

In an August 2007 article titled "How Did Elvis Get Turned Into a Racist?" Guralnick expressed puzzlement as to why Elvis Presley is considered by many in the contemporary African-American community to have been a racist. In fact, he was a strong supporter of black music. Guralnick said, "It was in his embrace of black music that Elvis came in for his fiercest criticism." Billboard editor Paul Ackerman recalled that, in 1958, calls poured in to insist that Billboard stop listing Presley's records on the best-selling country chart because he played black music.

Presley gave blues singer Arthur Crudup, who originated "That's All Right, Mama," the credit for his own success. Crudup used to "bang his box the way I do now, and I said if I ever got to the place where I could feel all old Arthur felt, I'd be a music man like nobody ever saw."

Presley and Charles had parallel lives during the 1960s, with both of them hitting number one on the charts. Presley died of a drug overdose in 1977.

In 1961, Ray Charles met Joe Adams, who was a well-known radio and television personality. The two men struck up a friendship, and Charles ended up bring Adams on as his manager. Adams stayed on as manager for the rest of Charles's career—over four decades. Adams is shown second from right in this 1964 photograph.

country and western album; *Modern Sounds in Country and Western Music* went to number one on the album charts. In an article called "Why Ray Charles Matters," Robert Lashley wrote,

> The enduring theme of the *Modern Sounds of County and Western* volumes isn't that music has no category, but that all music's categories are under the umbrella of and should be subservient to great art. Both albums [*Genius Hits the Road* and *Modern Sounds*] are the sound of a gifted man stretching his gifts beyond depths he can't imagine.

Charles recorded a song called "I Can't Stop Loving You," and it soared to number one on the charts. As many as 20,000 people were turning out at concerts. He took the band back to France, and his French fans went wild once again. Crowds stood in the rain for hours in Brussels, Belgium, to see "the genius," and German audiences also turned out in droves. Charles was so rich now that he bought another plane for his entourage of musicians, who had previously been bused to national gigs. When he played at the Latin Casino in Cherry Hill, New Jersey, Charles's fee was $25,000. He quickly went into production for *Modern Sounds in Country and Western Music Volume Two*, which, although considered inferior to the first recording, managed to stay on the charts for 67 weeks. *Billboard* saluted Charles as the number one recording artist of 1962.

In the winter of 1963, Charles talked to Joe Adams about moving his corporation to Los Angeles. After two close calls flying, he decided that they wouldn't fly in winter. Instead, he would use those months to record and run his business.

Adams started to run the band, taking care of the day-to-day activities. Jeff Brown knew that his days were limited. Charles had never given him the promised money from Tangerine Records, and his salary had barely changed over the years. Milt Shaw and Charles's promoter, Hal Zeiger, often sent checks to Brown, as they thought Charles's treatment of him was unfair.

A FAMILY AFFAIR

The band members knew that Joe Adams did not like musicians, and they did not like him, either. Adams encouraged Charles to fire musicians who didn't play by the rules. Still, Charles somehow managed to create a symbiotic relationship with the band and with the Raelettes. He expected everyone to work as hard as he did, and most met the challenge. Outsiders were amazed at how Charles managed to develop such a close family feeling in the touring company. Musician Hank Crawford said that Charles had them spellbound: "He was a general! And blind! He was young but we followed him as an older person." Things worked smoothly, everyone learned soon enough, as long as Charles was in charge.

Charles's next idea was to create an album that would paint the emotion of "soul." Nat Hentoff quoted poet James Baldwin in an article he wrote for the *Sunday Times*, "The blues and spirituals are all about . . . the ability to look at things as they are and survive your losses, or not even survive them—to know your losses are coming. Charles sings a kind of universal blues. It is not self-pity, however, which you hear in him, but compassion." Charles brought in Sid Feller, an old friend, to help with the arrangements, and the resulting album, *Ingredients in a Recipe for Soul,* was first class. He included songs such as "Over the Rainbow" and "Born to Be Blue."

A couple of glitches occurred in an otherwise smooth-running life. Charles had a brief relationship with a woman named Sandra Jean Betts, which resulted in Betts getting pregnant. Betts talked to lawyers and decided to file a complaint against Charles to establish patrimony. This would force Charles to provide support for her baby, soon to be born out of wedlock. Charles saw it as legal blackmail and refused to comment. Betts and her lawyer held their ground. It would be a long drawn-out battle, and even after the baby girl was born, Charles would not back down. Following that, Louise

DID YOU KNOW?

Using a computer program that he created to break down Ray Charles's rendition of "Fever," Southern Oregon University information scientist and music expert Ken Lindsay discovered that Charles's finger snaps set the main beat with an accuracy of two and a half milliseconds—half the time it takes a honeybee to flap its wings once. Lindsay said that Charles's ability to control rhythm was "incredible."

Mitchell, Charles's first love, went after him for support for her daughter, 13-year-old Evelyn. Charles invited Evelyn to come visit him and promised to send more money, which appeased Mitchell.

In the meantime, Joe Adams helped Charles find property in Los Angeles that would eventually become his foundation. Once built, it would become Charles's true home on earth, according to his biographer Michael Lydon: "The building he built there, its offices, recording studio, and bachelor pad, became his castle, his fortress, his faraway island; the place where he could work and play and live and love and be by himself whenever he pleased."

In 1963, for the first time in nine years, record sales all over were starting to drop. Charles's albums and singles didn't have quite as much appeal to blacks, who had shifted their interest to B.B. King and James Brown. Charles's singles sales had dropped to fourth place after the Beach Boys, Dion, and the Four Seasons. Elvis Presley had a total of 17 number-one hits that year, while Charles only had 3. None of it mattered that much to Charles. He and his band were about to circle the globe on their next tour.

7

The Roller Coaster Years

The start of the new year was far from auspicious. The *Betts v. Robinson* paternity trial started in Los Angeles on January 13, 1964. The jury ruled in favor of Betts, and Charles was ordered to pay child support. Charles's wife, Della Robinson, hated all the publicity because it exposed her strange marital situation. Charles, however, went on to make a new album, putting it all behind him.

That year, the Beatles stormed the United States. Their songs "I Want to Hold Your Hand," "Can't Buy Me Love," and "Twist and Shout" shot to the top of the charts. Soon, the Rolling Stones, the Animals, and the Dave Clark Five were topping the charts as American popular music underwent another radical change, which would become known as the British Invasion. These British bands had been listening to American rock and roll for almost a decade and had adapted the rhythms to their taste. At the young age of 34, Charles was becoming an old-timer—but he was not about to go quietly.

Ertegun and Wexler were excited that the records they had recorded with Charles, which they still owned, were being played more than his new recordings made for ABC. Wexler began to claim publicly that Charles's new music had lost the raw edge that made it so special. Other publications joined in and subtly echoed Wexler. The general consensus was that Charles had sold out when he shifted his focus to pop music.

Work was Charles's way of coping with his problems and with his triumphs. If he was in a downswing, the situation could change overnight. He had always maintained that there was no way a musician could tell which songs would appeal to the public. It was a mystery to everyone in the business, which was what made it risky.

Heroin had started to affect Charles's voice by the mid-1960s, making it more manic than ever, but his live audiences did not seem to mind. His 1964 album, *Sweet and Sour Tears*, was viewed as a failure, but still, as critic Robert Lashley wrote, "Its overall madness and pathos take hold."

THE FINAL BUST

After another long tour that included Australia, Charles returned to Los Angeles to a grand new home and to 2107 West Washington in Los Angeles, the new complex of buildings that housed Ray Charles Enterprises. He barely had time to settle in before he and the 25-member band were touring again, this time heading east. They went from Cleveland to Montreal to Boston. Once he was at the hotel in Boston, Charles realized that he had left his stash of drugs on the plane. It surprised many that he went back to get it, but he had a rule that no one carried for him unless they were carrying for themselves.

Customs officials had made note of the planeload of blacks arriving in Boston. Two policemen, Joseph J. Lally and Arthur Fitzgerald, thought it suspicious when they saw Charles and his driver, Clarence Driver (his real name), show up at 5:30 in the morning. They watched as Charles and Driver entered the plane and emerged 20 minutes later. Lally and Fitzgerald asked them to come to the customs office, where they asked Charles why he had returned to the plane. The response was, "To get a book."

They asked to see Charles's overcoat, in which they found a jar full of pot and Charles's heroin, along with the utensils needed for taking the drugs. When asked, Charles said that the powder was for his stomach. After hours of questioning, Charles was released on his own recognizance and went back to the hotel. He was furious with himself and deeply worried. He was dealing with the federal government this time—*United States of America v. Ray Charles.* Customs impounded Charles's plane and found more drugs. Although he somehow stayed cool on the surface, Charles was filled with anxiety. He went ahead with his concert, and the drug bust story appeared in national papers the following morning. The *Indianapolis Recorder* headline read, "Ray Charles Faces 40 Years on Dope Rap."

From then on, all was chaos. College bookers canceled, as were gigs to which Charles had planned to fly. During this uproar, Jeff Brown wrote his letter of resignation. Charles had been phasing him out for a long time as Joe Adams took over. Brown felt that he was good mainly for Charles's honesty, and Charles did not want that.

Charles made a big decision: They would play one more concert in Brooklyn, after which he and the band would go home to Los Angeles. He would not tour in 1965. He had been "gigging" for nine months out of the year for a long time, and it was time to slow down.

The weeks dragged by. One day, Tom Dowd, Charles's audio engineer from Atlantic Records, was in town and gave Charles a call. Charles asked him to come right over. All the new equipment was tangled up, and Charles did not know what to do. Dowd fixed the problem, and they sat down to work. By the time Dowd left, everything in the studio was perfect and

Ray Charles's studio, RPM International, was completed in 1964. Charles built the studio after he won his first Grammy Awards. Charles's final public appearance, in April 2004, took place at the dedication of his studio as a historic landmark.

Charles was deeply grateful. The hours they spent together must have been tinged with nostalgia for the old days.

Charles missed the touring routine, which had never been broken before. It felt strange not to be gigging. Looking at the calendar, 1965 was blank, and troubles kept coming in the front door. In January, Milt Shaw's mother died. Charles was high when he attended the funeral with Shaw. ABC-Paramount's new president, Sam Clark, worried about the trouble his star was in. He also worried that Charles would not sound as good off heroin as he did on it.

That year, Nat "King" Cole died, Malcolm X was shot to death, and Mae Mosely Lyles went to court to try to get $2,000 a month to support her child. Charles refused, and a trial date was set. Many thought Charles should have settled with her and not allowed the case to go public, but Charles's stubborn streak took over.

The drug bust overshadowed everything else. A criminal indictment went out against Charles on four narcotics charges for possessing heroin and marijuana and bringing the drugs into the country. As usual, Charles let his lawyers worry about it and began to set up his new office.

Charles named his complex, which consisted of recording, publishing, and management, the RPM International Building. It housed Tangerine Records, Tangerine Music, and Racer Music Company. He had a dozen employees working there. It was a dream come true to have his own studio.

Five of the 12 tracks of his new album—*Country and Western Meets Rhythm and Blues*—belonged to Tangerine Records. Charles was quite wealthy, mostly because of his business sense and his fearlessness when it came to asking for what he wanted. The $100,000 renewal contract he and Adams ended up getting from ABC-Paramount was just one example.

After signing in New York, Charles flew to Boston and pleaded not guilty to the charges against him. If convicted on all four counts, he could end up spending 60 years in jail. It was hinted that Charles would get a lighter sentence if he named his dealers, but he refused. The question was put to him: In exchange for a lighter sentence, would he give up heroin? Though he did not commit then, it made him think. Around the same time, Mae Mosely Lyles won her suit, which again upset Della Robinson because of the publicity, but Charles could hardly be bothered. He would pay.

GIVING UP HEROIN

The looming question was, what was he going to do about his heroin use? He knew that there would be more busts if he continued to use, and he knew what had happened to great musicians and singers like Billie Holliday and Charlie Parker—both had died of heroin overdoses. His buddy Fathead Newman was about to go to prison in Texas because of heroin. Michael Lydon wrote, "Heroin or music, that's what it came down to. . . . It would be crazy . . . worse, it would be stupid to throw away music for a drug." In addition, Charles worried about losing his children's love and respect if he went to prison.

Ray Charles and Politics

Although Charles seemed apolitical most of his life, the album he created in 1972 tells a different story. He wanted to record music for that album, *A Message From the People*, according to his biographer Michael Lydon, that was what "you might call a little militant, saying some of the wrong things that were happening in the country." He wanted the album to be a picture of him with children of all races, looking upward at the faces of Abraham Lincoln, Martin Luther King Jr., John F. Kennedy Jr., and Robert F. Kennedy. The first song on the album was the Negro national anthem, "Lift Every Voice and Sing." To balance some of the more strident "message" songs, Charles included songs that showed that he loved America. He ended the album with "America the Beautiful," arranged by Quincy Jones. The album did not sell well.

Charles did take a stand against segregated dance rooms but was careful about choosing sides in politics. Lydon said, "He avoided close contact with Martin Luther King or civil rights politics. 'I am an entertainer,' he said many times, 'a musician, not a politician.'" He did not like political benefits, either. His agent, Larry Myers, recalled Charles telling him that "when the stagehands and ushers work for nothing, that's when I'll work for nothing."

When Ronald Reagan was reelected in 1984, Democrats were furious over his policies, which they believed excluded blacks, rolled back civil rights, and made the rich richer. It was a shock that Charles sang at the Republican Convention when Reagan's nomination was announced. The rumor went around that he was a black conservative, kowtowing to the Republicans, who did not support blacks. Charles was angry when confronted about his choice, responding that "the Democrats wanted me to play the same thing, but they didn't want to pay." He again reiterated that he was "a person who plays music, and I'll take my music anywhere in the world people want to hear it."

As if to prove a point, in January 1993, he sang "America the Beautiful" for President Bill Clinton's inaugural gala at the Lincoln Memorial. In the fall of that year President Clinton awarded him the National Medal of Arts.

Alone, Charles reached a decision. He went to Joe Adams's office and announced that he was checking into a hospital. He was done with heroin. Charles insisted on kicking his habit cold turkey, but he wanted to do it in a hospital. His lawyers found a doctor named Frederick Hacker, who had a thriving celebrity business. Hacker came through, and, on July 26, Charles's valet, Vernon Troupe, drove him to the hospital. It was as if he had disappeared into thin air.

At the hospital, Charles refused all drugs that might help him. It was awful. He vomited over and over again, and it was rumored that he was dying of cancer. Dr. Hacker announced that Charles could not stand to go through a trial for at least nine weeks. Charles met with Hacker three times a week to talk, and eventually a bond grew between them. Hacker listened as Charles delved into the painful times of his childhood. Charles acknowledged that he resented being forced to give up heroin, but there was no way around it.

A DAUNTING CHALLENGE

Della Robinson visited Charles at the hospital and brought some food. After a while, Charles began to make calls to his office. Hacker allowed Charles to visit girlfriends and then came up with the idea of teaching Charles to play chess. Charles had insomnia, and he and another patient began to play through the night. Charles felt the pieces before and after every move, and although he always lost, he persisted. He said he loved chess because "with cards, no matter how well you play, you ain't gonna win unless the cards fall for you. But in chess, it my brain against yours! We start with the same pieces in the same places. . . . You've got to outwit, out-think, and out-maneuver the other person, and he's thinking how to outwit you." Lydon thought of chess as a perfect metaphor for Charles's life: "attack and retreat, hide and dare, plan five moves ahead."

In order to break his addiction to heroin, Charles solicited the help of Dr. Frederick Hacker. Hacker taught Charles how to play chess, an activity he kept up with for the rest of his life. Charles played the game on a board with special niches so that he could feel the position of the pieces.

Charles started to record again in October even as his lawyers were still bargaining with the prosecutors. In November, Charles pleaded guilty. The defense lawyers brought in Dr. Hacker, who talked about Charles's cure. Knowing that time would tell, the judge, with Charles's permission, extended the case for a year, during which time Charles would agree to examinations by government doctors. Charles was happy. He knew he would not go back to heroin, which meant that he would not have to go to prison. Charles always maintained that Dr. Frederick Hacker had saved his life.

Charles's valet, Vernon Troupe, found the change in him amazing. He was much warmer and enjoyed kidding around. Troupe was glad to have the old Charles gone, and so was everyone else. Despite kicking his heroin addiction, Charles never considered giving up cigarettes or marijuana.

Charles wrote a song called "Crying Time" in 1965, and before it was released, he knew that he had another strong single. He also knew that he had lost ground while he was away. A new era was dawning, and those at the top of the charts were a decade younger. He went right to work on a new album, *Ray's Moods*. The single "Crying Time" went to number six on the charts in the beginning of 1966. It was Charles's biggest hit in two years.

In April 1967, Charles was ordered to fly to Boston for drug testing. He was pronounced clean. The following weekend, he earned $68,000 from three gigs. In May, his song "Let's Go Get Stoned" started to climb the charts. It was assumed to be Charles getting back at the authorities, but it wasn't funny when, on June 12, Milt Shaw was found dead of a heroin overdose in his apartment. It marked the end of the Shaw legacy.

A seven-page spread in *Life Magazine* entitled "Music Soaring in a Darkened World . . . The Comeback of Ray Charles," came out in July 1969. In it, Frank Sinatra was quoted as saying that "Ray Charles is the only genius in our business." Charles was at the top of his form, as was his band. To date, he had created 30 albums and at least double that many singles. From live shows alone in 1966, he had brought in $750,000.

Charles had to appear in court once more because of the heroin arrest. The old judge had died, but he had left instructions: If Charles was clean, he was to be fined $10,000 and given two-year probation. Elated, Charles and the band flew back to Los Angeles, where Charles spent time with his wife and his boys. In 1967, he started hosting Sunday chess matches at home, and his wife would serve food and drinks. Back at work on Monday, he and Sid Feller created a new album, *Ray Charles Invites You to Listen*. Then it was off to Europe again. The reviews on his return were unfavorable, insinuating that the style of the music was old-fashioned. Joe Adams thought that Charles needed to get some positive headlines, so he arranged for Charles to become national chairman of the Sickle Cell Anemia Research Foundation (sickle cell anemia is an illness that affects mainly blacks) and then had the mayor of Los Angeles declare June 8 to be "Ray Charles Day."

Popular music was undergoing many changes. The Beatles returned to the United States with *Sgt. Pepper's Lonely Hearts Club Band*, and Bob Dylan, the Beach Boys, and other groups were taking the nation by storm. Among black singers, Aretha Franklin was making her way to stardom. Charles recorded the Beatles' hit "Yesterday" to great acclaim.

A new gig lay just ahead: the Copacabana, a swanky club in New York City that until then had been off-limits to Charles because of his drug busts. He packed the place, two shows nightly and three on weekends. It was there that he met Arlette Kotchounian, a photographer from Paris, who managed to get backstage to bring a translation of a song she liked ("The Sun Died") to Charles. He liked it, and he liked her. She would remain in his life for many years.

Charles signed on with the William Morris Agency. His first gig under them was to sing at the Coconut Grove at the Ambassador Hotel in Florida.

The Raelettes rebelled about their pay during this period. Charles fired their leader, Gwen Berry, and the others resigned. He replaced them with a new group including Susaye Green, an 18-year-old soprano, who was given a solo spot. She became Charles's "first lady of the moment." The new Raelettes were a handful, constantly squabbling and competing for his attention. Charles pleaded with old friend Mable John, a blues singer from Detroit, to come on board as a soloist and to take charge of the girls. Knowing that Charles would be cheap if she let him, she delivered a contract that would work for her, and Charles agreed.

Charles did not stop creating new albums as the 1960s drew to a close. *I'm All Yours, Baby* was a romance album, and it was followed by an R&B album, *Doing His Thing*. Some critics thought that they were full of gimmicks. Sales were down, but Charles continued in his usual pattern: creating albums that he liked, touring, and meeting with his women. All he needed was another hit.

8

Learning to Diversify

What was different this time around was that the lull continued. Charles was in a pattern that others who had experienced phenomenal success had also been through. They would attempt to repeat the same successful pattern, making each year equally profitable. Invariably, they would become invisible, and all they could do was keep working and hoping that they would be seen with a new eye. A retired record executive said, "There comes a point in nearly every artist's career when he or she stops selling records. They may be great, but the market moves past them."

Things were uneasy with ABC, but Charles continued to record albums in his studio. *My Kind of Jazz* and *Love Country Style* were the result. He was sounding imitative again. The former reminded audiences of Count Basie, and the latter had a strong Nashville sound.

During this time, Charles met another woman, Ruth Robinson, who, like so many others, fell in love with him. Charles had started a new habit of drinking all day, and he taught Robinson to make his "special" coffee each morning: fill a coffee mug halfway with coffee and then to the top with gin. When he flew to Los Angeles between gigs it was to see Robinson. Sometimes his wife and children did not even know he had been there.

The recording process was changing again. Overdubbing basic records was the new style of creating records, which made the finished product more like a collage, as pieces were added from numerous sessions. Charles could work on several albums simultaneously, assembling them piecemeal. He called in old friend Sid Feller to play with him in the studio as he decided what to produce next. No one denied that Charles could be difficult, but most kept working with him. Feller said to a fellow musician who complained about Charles, "Ray can be a pain in the neck. If you didn't like him, you'd leave him."

All the press releases issued around this time announced that Charles was celebrating his twenty-fifth year in show business in 1971. The year opened with him performing for Quincy Jones in a work called "Black Requiem," written by Jones. Charles then joined Aretha Franklin, an up-and-coming star, on stage at the Fillmore in San Francisco for a duet of the song "Spirit in the Dark." Franklin's album of the show became a hit, and Charles profited.

Charles's Tangerine Records produced his album *Volcanic Actions of My Soul*. His maturity was obvious, and his songs, according to Michael Lydon, "convey a profound insight into the human spirit, a knowledge of life tempered by sympathy, patience, and sensual vigor—the qualities of a master." *A Message From the People* was Charles's next album, and it was not as appreciated at first as it would come to be years later. Both *Volcanic Actions of My Soul* and *A Message From the People* peaked on the charts at number 52.

Members of Charles's inner circle came and went. David "Fathead" Newman finally left for good to play for double the salary he received from Charles. Raelette Stella Yarborough was fired, and Charles brought back Dorothy Berry. Valets came and went, as did the women.

Joe Adams was the constant. He was not going to let happen to him what had happened to Jeff Brown. He kept a vigilant watch over everything and everyone to make certain that Charles had nothing to complain about, eventually making himself indispensable. Charles was responsible for a lot of people, and sometimes it weighed heavily on him. He continued to sip his gin and coffee throughout the day.

At this point in his life, Charles looked like a light-heavyweight boxer. He had broad shoulders and narrow hips and legs. His head hung forward when he walked on the arm of his valet, entering unknown territory. He smiled broadly, and for shows, he dressed in a bright blue tuxedo. When he stepped onstage, he performed his customary action of wrapping both arms tightly around his body. Audiences loved it.

CHANGE IN FOCUS

Even with the shows he was doing, Charles was in a slump. Critics continued to say that he seemed too far out of touch with contemporary trends. Jon Landau wrote in *Rolling Stone* magazine that Charles "has coasted continually without ever progressing beyond the style and sound that made him famous." Jay Lasker, the head of ABC-Paramount, decided to let Charles go after 14 years. At the advice of a friend, Charles changed the name of his company from Tangerine Records to Crossover. After cutting a new album titled *Come Live With Me* without ABC distributing for him, he realized that he was truly on his own. Although his fellow musicians predicted that the album would be a big hit, it flopped.

He decided to focus on touring. He still had a big band that resembled those of the 1930s. It was divided into four

Ray Charles basks in the welcome accorded him at a jazz festival in Boston in 1993. Throughout his life, Charles was grateful to his audiences, and they repaid him with enthusiasm.

sections that consisted of a rhythm section (including drums, double bass, guitar, and keyboard instruments) and saxophone, trombone, and trumpet sections. The members had to be excellent musicians, for Charles was demanding and hard to follow. Musician John Bryant said, "To play with Ray, you had to be good enough to play with Count Basie, but Count

Basie spoke through his band. Ray's band *served* Ray. He was the focus."

The reports from musicians were contradictory, with more complaints than compliments during this era. Part of the problem was Joe Adams's admitted dislike of musicians. Charles considered band members his employees. Lydon wrote, "Ray projected a distant, disdainful attitude to the band members. 'Like we were cattle,' one put it." The biggest complaint was still how stingy he was, yet for many of the newcomers, especially the young single men, it was the best salary they had ever made.

There was another part of Charles they all admired deeply— his art. Their loyalty was about more than money. After traveling with Charles for nine months across many countries, Leroy Cooper confessed to Michael Lydon,

> For nine months, I'd been getting a musical charge from hearing Ray. Sitting there night after night, hearing him sing, sometimes I'd be in tears and never let anybody know. Now I was headed back to Washington for the winter, and I'd get this sick feeling that I was going to be away from all that music for three long months to the spring.

The turnover of those close to Charles continued. Mable John did a great job with the Raelettes, who called her "Mother Superior." Then, one night at a concert in the mid 1970s, she heard a voice telling her to "go home." She enrolled in the Crenshaw Christian Center school and earned a doctorate. She started a mission in Los Angeles and stayed in touch with Charles for the rest of his life. Susaye Green took off in 1973 to sing with Stevie Wonder, another blind musician who made it to the top. David Braithwaite, who had worked for years as Charles's chief engineer, decided to leave, and Charles was too proud to ask him to come back. Charles bought an electronic synthesizer, and, on his next album, *Renaissance,* the

In the 1970s, Ray Charles still had a big band similar to those of the 1930s, with four sections: rhythm, drums, the saxophone, and horns. Here, Charles appears with his band in 1970, along with the four female singers known as the Raelettes.

synthesizer helped to bring Charles up to date on his sound. Still, the album only peaked at number 178 on the charts.

Della Robinson filed for divorce in 1976, but this time the details were kept out of the press. Ray Charles Jr. and his girlfriend lived with Robinson. Charles refused when Ray Jr. asked to work with him and instead kept his son on a modest allowance while he was at Whittier College, where he made average grades. His second son, David, ran with a wild crowd, and it was too early to tell about the youngest, Robert. Arlette Kotchounian had a son named Vincent by Charles, and another French woman gave birth to a daughter. Evelyn, Charles's first child, was a 27-year-old nurse and often received expensive gifts from her father.

By 1977, Charles had not had a hit in a decade. He was feisty though, as always, claiming that he did not like rock music and complaining that young players did not take the time to learn their instruments. He was adamant that artists had to control the commercial pressure put on them, not let it control them, although few adhered to that philosophy.

In a surprise move, Charles went to Ahmet Ertegun and Jerry Wexler at Atlantic Records to ask them for help. Atlantic was by then a successful corporation with major rock stars under its wing. The two men knew Charles's situation but still admired him. Charles suggested a deal whereby he would own his masters and would be able to put Crossover's label on the record jacket with Atlantic's. The two producers agreed.

Charles was invited to make appearances on various television shows, and although these appearances did not increase his record sales, they provided a financial cushion for him as people bought the old albums and went to his shows. Americans were listening to disco, and when Charles sent Ertegun the tracks for his new album, *True to Life*, Ertegun did not like them because they sounded old-fashioned. Charles refused to follow Ertegun's suggestions for change, though, and Ertegun released it the way it was. What was obvious, and sad, was that Charles was trying to be commercial, presenting a variety of songs that he hoped would please an audience he no longer knew.

In the meantime, David Ritz had come to Charles and asked to write his autobiography, an "as told to" book. Joe Adams did not like the idea, but Charles did, and he and Ritz got to work. When it was finished, the editors at Prentice Hall said that it had to be revised because of the profanity and rawness of the material. Charles refused to change anything and sold the manuscript to another press. When it was published in 1978, it had strong sales and good reviews. Some of his friends were hurt that they had either been left out or given short shrift, though. Upon reading the book, it is said, Joe Adams said, "I work for the man for twenty-five years, and that's all he has to say about me?" He then hurled his copy across the room.

A BITTER PHASE

As the 1970s drew to a close, it must have been painful for Charles to evaluate the past decade. He was divorced from his wife and he felt like he was on the sidelines of the music industry. He was desperate for a hit, but every new release died an early death. Even the touring had a sad edge to it as he found himself at Holiday Inns with half a roomful of people. He was embarrassed to play at the Coconut Grove for a fundraiser and realized that the place was almost empty. Asked by a reporter if it was hard to keep going, he replied, "There's times when all you have left between you and madness or even death is a kind of empty will."

Everyone noticed that Charles was more demanding than usual and quite irritable. His old valet, Vernon Troupe, said, "Ray's just the kind of person, you shove him in the corner, and he'll cut off his nose to spite his face." Charles refused to give raises, mentioning the amount of alimony he had to pay out and the number of people he had to take care of. He told Susaye Green one day that he did not have any dreams anymore. Green said that Charles ended up in a time warp, unlike his friends Quincy Jones and Stevie Wonder, who kept adapting to the new trends.

There were some good moments. The Georgia House of Representatives declared "Georgia on My Mind" the state song. Charles flew to Atlanta to sing it, deeply moved to be recognized by the state of his birth. The gigs continued to be depressing, however, as Charles had not invested in any of rock's big electric sound systems, which made his band sound thin. One player, Harold Patton, decided to quit, saying that the atmosphere in the band had passed beyond nasty to mean. The feeling of family was gone.

By 1980, Charles's hair was completely gray and his face creased; he looked old before his time. He was at the lowest

America the Beautiful

Charles and his trio had played in Dallas on September 10, 2001, the night before the World Trade Center was hit in the 9/11 attacks. They were at the airport the following morning when they saw on television what was going on. Three days later, Charles was finally able to fly to L.A. He and the band had a gig in Newark, New Jersey, on September 17. As they closed the show, drummer Pete Turre played the opening drum roll to "America the Beautiful." Turre explained what happened: "The people knew what was coming and went absolutely nuts, clapping and screaming. They went dead silent while Ray sang, but at the final chorus, everybody was singing along except they were bawling so hard they could hardly sing. I was crying too, couldn't help it."

Charles's version of "America the Beautiful" had been recorded 30 years before on his album *A Message From the People*. As usual with Charles, it was a unique version: He begins the song with the third verse.

In 1976, at a Carnegie Hall concert, Charles asked the audience to join in. As the lights came up, a huge American flag unfurled above the stage, and the audience leapt to its feet. In 1998, he performed the song at a naturalization ceremony on Ellis Island in New York.

Lynn Sherr, a correspondent for the ABC News program *20/20* wrote a book entitled *America the Beautiful: The Stirring True Story Behind Our Nation's Favorite Song*. She told *New York Times* reporter Clyde Haberman that "this is the original optimistic vision of America. It's a hymn. It's an anthem. It so captures the American spirit in a way that no other song does. It always makes me proud."

Sherr called the song the "national heartbeat set to music." Ray Charles saw it that way, too. He was quoted in her book as saying, "Honestly, wouldn't you rather sing about the beauty of America?"

On a less noble note, after 2001, people going up the stairs at the Resorts International Casino in Atlantic City would be met with "Ray Charles—America the Beautiful" slot machines. They cost a nickel to play, and the wheels showed pianos, sunglasses, and records. A plastic Ray Charles doll that nodded its head and played bits of "What'd I Say" and "America the Beautiful" was nearby.

A lot of controversy existed around Charles's willingness to perform the song at both Republican and Democratic conventions, but Charles ignored the criticism and went on his way. "America the Beautiful" was performed at his funeral.

point in his career. He appeared in a film titled *The Blues Brothers* with *Saturday Night Live* stars John Belushi and Dan Aykroyd. The film was extremely popular and reintroduced Charles to the younger crowd. He made a fourth album for Atlantic called *Brother Ray Is at It Again,* which again did not go anywhere. Ertegun was ready to call it quits.

PERSEVERANCE

Charles refused to accept defeat. He had to change, and he finally did by diversifying. Along with television appearances, he began to perform with symphony orchestras. An evening with the Boston Pops was broadcast on PBS television, and Ray Charles was recognized by a new audience. He had created concert programs for a string and woodwind orchestra, which meant that he did not have to pay phenomenal sums of money to take a band around the country; instead, he was in charge of five people. He started to receive $50,000 per performance for gigs for corporations and other private groups.

By 1980, he still did not have a contract with a label company. In 1981, he played at the Grand Ole Opry, singing with Loretta Lynn, and the crowd loved it. Charles decided to make country music his focus. The Nashville sound had grown and become extremely popular at this time. It took seven months of talks for Rick Blackburn, head of CBS Records' country division, to come to an agreement. Charles was feeling upbeat again; he had a new sound. Blackburn released "Born to Love Me" in December, and it climbed to number 20 on the country chart. In 1983, Ray completed another album, *Wish You Were Here Tonight,* and suddenly he had top billing at the Country Music Association's 25th Anniversary Concert in Washington, D.C., attended by President Reagan and his wife. It was not a great album, but it became a moderate hit.

Then, bad luck struck again: One of Charles's ears stopped functioning. He heard only echo sounds and worried that he was going deaf. He was diagnosed with "abnormally patent

Eustachian tubes." A specialist made an opening in his eardrum and put in a ventilating tube. It got infected, and Charles almost died, but antibiotics saved him.

The 1983 tour was the worst in band members' memory. Joe Adams had installed a new road manager who was worse than Adams himself. One of the band members finally confronted Charles in the middle of a concert and was dismissed. Charles continued to tour and record.

He went to Nashville and met Billy Sherrill, a top producer. Charles talked to him about creating an album of duets, and they started to organize it. Some of the players in Nashville had long worshipped Charles, which gave him a boost. He sang with Merle Haggard, Ricky Skaggs, and Willie Nelson. The album, called *Friendship*, was declared a masterpiece.

Work was more than ever the core of Charles's life. He continued to tour, taking his music to the people. Joe Adams and Charles were still a team, and Charles had the same bookkeeper for three decades. Della Robinson and Charles were on better terms. Ray Jr., however, now a father with two children, was having trouble with his marriage. He had never gotten his feet on the ground, always hoping that his father would let him be his right-hand man. Charles's second son, David, became deeply involved in drugs and suffered from hallucinations. He was accused of sexually assaulting two women at gunpoint and pleaded guilty to two counts of rape. He was sent to prison for 11 years. Robert, the youngest, was hoping to be a minister. For his part, although Charles had not been there as his children grew up, he was disappointed in them. Some thought that his secretiveness kept him from allowing his sons into his business and into his life.

A CELEBRITY

In the process of reinventing himself, Charles had become a celebrity at age 55. It was a mixed blessing: Although his "appearances" brought in a lot of money, he was being recognized for gimmicks rather than for his art. The venues, instead of being concerts that displayed his phenomenal talent, were television talk shows and White House appearances. He sang at Ronald Reagan's second inaugural gala, where he was introduced by Frank Sinatra. In 1986, he guest-starred on *Who's the Boss* and *Designing Women*, and he appeared with Madonna on the *Johnny Carson Show*.

He could not be a celebrity without a certain number of recent successes. The duet with Willie Nelson from *Friendship*, "Seven Spanish Angels," had gone to number one on the country charts. He also was invited to join Bob Dylan, Diana Ross, Bruce Springsteen, and 40 other famous pop singers to sing "We Are the World," which was a huge success.

In 1987, Charles decided he wanted to create the Robinson Foundation for Hearing Disorders and donated $250,000 in the first year to get it started. In August, he was selected to receive the Kennedy Center Honors Medal, America's most distinguished award for the arts. At the ceremony, Stevie Wonder sang a medley of songs, film clips of Charles's life were shown, and a chorus from the Florida School for the Deaf and Blind sang "America the Beautiful." Charles admitted to being overjoyed. He next received a Lifetime Achievement Award from the National Academy of Recording Arts and Sciences.

In his mid-50s, Ray was in perpetual motion, according to his new valet, Dave Simmons, and he was "tiny," with broad shoulders and a small waist. He was treated like royalty wherever he went, as most celebrities are. Charles, however, was demanding of everyone around him and impatient to the point of cruelty with musicians who could not "get it right." His voice was in excellent form during these years. Sax player Rudy Johnson said of Charles during this era, "Ray would do things with his voice so gorgeous that I'd think he would do them again, but no, just that one time!"

As Charles kept producing albums, Joe Adams was talking to Pepsi-Cola about having Charles do a series of ads. The

In the early 1990s, Charles won an endorsement deal with Pepsi, which popularized the phrase "You've got the right one, Baby." Here, he appears in one of the ads with the "Uh-Huh" girls.

famous advertising agency BBD&O agreed, and they filmed ads that featured Charles sparring with quarterback Joe Montana (who dazzled everyone with his skills at the Super Bowl in 1990 playing for the San Francisco 49ers). This was the boost that put Charles on top again. Already famous for his music, Charles became a celebrity icon, and the money from the ads poured into Ray Charles Enterprises. The second series of ads starring Charles were like small films. Dubbed the "uh-huh" commercials, they, according to biographer Lydon, proved that Charles's music was universal and that no one does it better. The main phrase in the commercials—"You've got the right one, Baby"—became an American catch phrase, making Ray Charles a hip star of the 1990s. Charles, however, sometimes felt that he had to remind people that "My thing goes way beyond the Pepsi commercial."

"I never wanted to be famous, but I always wanted to be great," Charles said many times over his lifetime. The irony was not lost on him that he was, at this stage of his life, one of the most recognized faces on the planet. He had earned his fame; he was not so sure about how he felt being a celebrity.

9

Legacy

The 2003 concert season was in full swing, and Charles was opening at the Resorts International Casino in Atlantic City. Looking like an old man, he did a rousing rendition of "What'd I Say" and the middle-aged audience loved it. At the end, as Joe Adams was about to whisk him off the stage, he said, "Thank you, thank you, people, there are no words to say how much I appreciate you staying with me through all these years." With that, he spread his arms wide, then wrapped his arms around his body, his signature way of bringing the people into his heart.

Shortly after that concert, in the middle of the tour, Joe Adams fired the road manager and sent a cold letter to the band members, saying that Charles's health—he needed a hip replacement—required him to cancel the rest of the season. They all went home puzzled. They knew it had to be more than the hip replacement; after all, Charles had not shut down his touring machine since 1965. Rumors began to fly. Finally, it was learned that Charles had terminal liver cancer and emphysema.

After Charles canceled his 2003 world tour, his ghostwriter and friend David Ritz called him. Charles sounded subdued and distracted. "My liver's not right," he told Ritz. "I'm not putting out no press release, but I heard them use the word 'cancer.'" His office continued to send out reports that he was planning a tour, but Ritz soon learned that the tour would not happen. When Charles called Ritz one day, Ritz dropped everything and immediately went to the studio. Charles was seated behind the control board, Ritz wrote,

> his fingers running up and down the switches of the elaborate recording console that anchored his musical life. He looked smaller, thinner, certainly diminished but far from defeated. . . . I thought of the hundreds of thousands of hours he had spent here—singing, writing, playing keyboards, rehearsing singers, musicians, mixing his songs, recording his voice. That voice, once an instrument of unprecedented power, was reduced to a whisper. . . . His robust frame had melted into the frail body of a sick old man.

It was obvious to Ritz that Charles was coming to terms with his impending death. Charles acknowledged in their conversation that he had hurt some musicians by "being too much in a hurry. Too impatient. Looking for everything to be perfect. Lost my head. I feel like I hurt people. I know I hurt people. . . . Tell them I have feelings too. I can feel their feelings, man. Tell them I appreciate them. Tell them. . . just tell them Brother Ray loves them." He began to cry and signaled Ritz to leave.

In April 2004, Ritz saw Charles again at a ceremony to commemorate Charles's Los Angeles studio as a historical monument. Charles emerged in a pin-striped suit, obviously in pain. He was lifted from the chair and brought to the podium, and

Joe Adams placed his hand over the plaque. Barely audible, Charles thanked the city for the honor. He struggled for breath and said, "I'm weak. But I'm getting stronger."

Ray Charles died on June 10. Ronald Reagan's funeral, which lasted for days, was still going on at that time. Although all the major newspapers had headlines on their front pages to announce Charles's death, Reagan's funeral dominated the news.

The Film *Ray*

Taylor Hackford spent 15 years trying to get Ray Charles's life story onto the big screen. As he started the process, executives were hesitant to put up the money, saying that "nobody remembers Charles," "young people aren't interested," and "African-American films don't sell overseas."

Hackford had to find money to make the film. A longtime fan of Ray Charles's music, Philip Anschutz, stepped up and offered to fund it. Because he was a religious conservative, he gave some conditions: no sex and no swearing. Hackford thought that would be impossible, but Anschutz now had the rights.

They remained at a stalemate until Charles stepped in, explaining to Hackford that he did not swear as much in the 1950s. Originally titled *Unchain My Heart* and later changed to *Ray*, it wound up being a sexy and tough film even without the graphic elements.

David Ritz, the ghostwriter for Charles's autobiography, was critical of the film. He felt that Hackford made the story sentimental. Still, the complexities of Charles's character come through in the film. He was presented as ruthless in business and addicted to women and drugs.

Hackford wanted Jamie Foxx to play Charles, but Charles insisted that first he and Foxx sit down to play piano together. They played for two hours, and at the end, Charles stood up and hugged Foxx. Hackford was aware that he was a white man directing a film about a black hero, but once Jamie Foxx signed on, it became a partnership. Raelette Stella Yarborough said that Foxx was a "dead ringer" for the young Ray Charles. Hackford also brought in black writer Jimmy White.

The film was released in 2004, shortly after Charles's death. The completed film was screened for Charles before he died. Foxx won an Oscar for his extraordinary performance, and four additional Oscars were presented to the producers. *Ray* was the third-highest DVD in sales in the United States in 2005.

Director Taylor Hackford wanted Jamie Foxx to play Ray Charles in the biopic *Ray*, but first Charles had to approve. Charles and Foxx developed a rapport after two hours of playing piano together, and many people thought that Foxx (above, as Charles) was a "dead ringer" for the young Ray Charles. Foxx won his first Oscar for his role in the 2004 film.

FUNERAL

Charles's body lay in state at the Los Angeles Convention Center. Thousands filed by. On June 18, he was buried at the First African Methodist Church in the South Central area of Los Angeles. The burial was an invitation-only affair. Wreaths to represent each of Charles's 12 children were placed around the walls of the mid-sized church. He had 21 grandchildren and 5 great-grandchildren. Susaye Green sang "The Lord's Prayer," and Fathead Newman, who had known Charles for 54 years, played "Precious Lord." Willie Nelson sang "Georgia on My Mind," B.B. King sang "Please Accept My Love," and Stevie Wonder played "I Won't Complain." The audience rose to its feet when he finished. "America the Beautiful" was played, and Wynton Marsalis played "Old Rugged Cross" and "Down by the Riverside" on trumpet.

LEGACY

When *New York Times* reporter Bob Herbert heard on the radio that Ray Charles had died, he wrote,

> For someone who had grown up with his music, as I had, who had gyrated to it in moments of fierce adolescent ecstasy, and listened to it with the volume turned low on some of those nights that no one should have to go through, it was like hearing about the death of a close friend who was both amazingly generous and remarkably wise.

Robert Lashley summed up Ray Charles's legacy in an article he wrote in 2005 titled "Why Ray Charles Matters." He said:

> So what are we to make of this great man? The answer's in the revolution he brought forth. Aretha Franklin and Otis Redding . . . kicked in the musical doors that Ray opened wide. . . . Sly Stone, Stevie Wonder, George Clinton and Prince took his fundamentals and added mind bending funk grooves to make the entire world their own personal revival meeting. You can also hear Charles in the rhythmic dynamic of later Beatles records. . . . And you can still hear his influence in Andre 3000's genre bending experiments, Jack White embracing the blues and country, Timbaland and Missy Elliot's everlasting search throughout the world for the perfect beat. . . .

Robert Lashley fully understood the meaning of what Charles was trying to do. He wrote:

> Charles's embrace of country [music] and its blood relationship to the nature of black music is seen by too many young African Americans as the move of a sellout. And in this era where a healthy response to political correctness has degenerated into a tacky soft core white nationalism,

In 1979, the Georgia State Assembly declared Ray Charles's version of "Georgia on My Mind" the official state song. Here, Charles smiles at the ovation he receives after the formal declaration is made.

Charles is seen by too many young whites as someone not to be taken seriously when you talk about the history of art in America. If we as a country don't absorb Charles's two great artistic themes, that art is a place where color plays no part and that the history of black music in America is one of the greatest things to ever happen in this country, we will lose a great deal of not just American music history, but American history as well.

Charles's old friend Quincy Jones was asked if there is a Ray Charles sound. "Absolutely," he said. "It is the pain converted into joy. It's darkness converted into light."

1930 Charles is born in Albany, Georgia.

1953 "Mess Around" is Charles's first big hit.

1955 "I Got a Woman" reaches the R&B chart.

1960 Charles wins four Grammy Awards for *Genius of Ray Charles* album, and "Let the Good Times Roll," "Georgia on My Mind, and "Hit the Road Jack."

1963 Charles wins Grammy for "Busted."

1967 Charles wins two Grammys for "Crying Time."

1971 Charles is celebrated with a Twenty-fifth Anniversary in Show Business Salute.

1976 Charles wins B'nai B'rith's Man of the Year in Los Angeles.

1979 Georgia State Music Hall of Fame recognizes Charles as a Georgia musician; "Georgia on My Mind" is made the official state song.

1980 *The Blues Brothers*, featuring Ray Charles, opens.

1981 Charles gets star on Hollywood Walk of Fame.

1986 Rock and Roll Hall of Fame inducts Charles; he receives the Kennedy Center Honors.

1988 Charles receives the Grammy Lifetime Achievement Award.

1991 Rhythm and Blues Foundation, Entertainment Hall of Fame, and the National Black Sports & Entertainment Hall of Fame induct Charles.

1993 Charles receives Lifetime Achievement Award from the Songwriters Hall of Fame; receives the National Medal of Arts.

1993 Charles wins his twelfth Grammy Award (Best Male R&B performance) for "Song for You."

1995   American Foundation for the Blind (AFB) presents
Charles with the first Helen Keller Personal Achievement Award.

1996   Charles receives an Honorary Doctorate in Performing Arts from Occidental College and a Horatio Alger
Award from the Association of Distinguished Americans.

2004   Charles dies on June 10; *Rolling Stone* magazine ranks
him number 10 on their list of the 100 Greatest Artists of All Time; his studio in Los Angeles is dedicated
as a historic landmark; Congress renames the former
West Adams Station Post Office in Los Angeles the "Ray
Charles Station"; the 2004 Grammy Awards Ceremony
is dedicated to Charles.

Charles, Ray, and David Ritz. *Brother Ray: Ray Charles' Own Story.* New York: DeCapo Press, 1978.

Floyd, Samuel A., Jr. *The Power of Black Music.* New York: Oxford University Press, 1995.

Guralnick, Peter. *Sweet Soul Music.* New York: Harper & Row, 1986.

Lydon, Michael. *Ray Charles: Man and Music.* New York, London: Routledge, 2004.

Wexler, Jerry, and David Ritz. *Rhythm and the Blues: A Life in American Music.* New York: Alfred A. Knopf, 1993.

WEB SITES

American Masters
http://www.pbs.org/wnet/americanmasters

Library of Congress, "Living Legends: Ray Charles"
http://loc.gov/about/awards/legends/bio/charles.html

Official Ray Charles Web site
http://raycharles.com

Rock and Roll Hall of Fame and Museum
http://rockhall.com

Soul-Patrol.com
http://www.soul-patrol.com

PAGE

Index

Janet Hubbard-Brown of Fayston, Vermont, is the author of numerous books for children and young adults, including biographies of such diverse people as Shirin Ebadi, Scott Joplin, Geoffrey Chaucer, and Condoleezza Rice. She particularly enjoyed writing *Ray Charles*; she saw him in concert twice and remains a fan. She also writes for magazines and is a freelance editor.